# NO APOLOGIES

# NO
## APOLOGIES

How to Find and Free Your Voice
in the Age of Outrage

*Lessons for the Silenced Majority*

Katherine Brodsky

PITCHSTONE PUBLISHING
DURHAM, NORTH CAROLINA

Pitchstone Publishing
Durham, North Carolina
www.pitchstonebooks.com

Library of Congress Cataloging-in-Publication Data

Names: Brodsky, Katherine, author.
Title: No apologies : how to find and free your voice in the age of outrage
  lessons for the silenced majority / Katherine Brodsky.
Description: Durham, North Carolina : Pitchstone Publishing, [2024] |
  Includes bibliographical references. | Summary: "In No Apologies,
  Katherine Brodsky argues that it's time for principled individuals to
  hit the unmute button and resist the authoritarians among us who name,
  shame, and punish. Recognizing that speaking authentically is easier
  said than done, she spent two years researching and interviewing those
  who have been subjected to public harassment and abuse for daring to
  transgress the new orthodoxy or criticize a new taboo. While she found
  that some of these individuals navigated the outrage mob better than
  others, and some suffered worse personal and professional effects than
  others, all of the individuals with whom she spoke remain unapologetic
  over their choice to express themselves authentically. In sharing their
  stories, which span the arts, education, journalism, and science,
  Brodsky uncovers lessons for all of us in the silenced majority to push
  back against the dangerous illiberalism of the vocal minority that
  tolerates no dissent- and to find and free our own voices"— Provided by
  publisher.
Identifiers: LCCN 2023041923 (print) | LCCN 2023041924 (ebook) | ISBN
  9781634312509 (cloth) | ISBN 9781634312516 (ebook)
Subjects: LCSH: Freedom of speech. | Intellectual freedom. | Dissenters. |
  BISAC: SELF-HELP / Personal Growth / General | FAMILY & RELATION-
SHIPS /
  General
Classification: LCC JC591 .B76 2024  (print) | LCC JC591  (ebook) | DDC
  323.44/3—dc23/eng/20231003
LC record available at https://lccn.loc.gov/2023041923
LC ebook record available at https://lccn.loc.gov/2023041924

# Contents

# Preface

I never planned to write this book—or any book, really. But one day, I realized that I could use the little voice that I do have to help others feel less alone—just as I, for a time, felt so alone in this mad, mad world.

I'm not so different from anyone else. My own struggle to liberate my voice—which for too long was suffocating under the weight of self-censorship—began in private and ended up culminating in an op-ed for *Newsweek*, in which I recounted my own encounter with the online mob and wrote the line that motivates this entire book: "When reasonable people stay silent, the voices of the unreasonable are allowed infinite room to fill the void."

But before discussing how I came to free my own voice, a bit of personal history should provide some important context. Although I am a Canadian citizen who has spent a lot of time in the United States, I was not born in Canada or the United States. I hail from the Soviet Union, where my family lived in full "glory" under its Communist regime. Like many Jewish families, we fled Ukraine with just about nothing in the midst of the ongoing Cold War, and even though I was just a child, the lessons of that period left a strong imprint on me, especially those related to the chilling effects of silencing and the damage that can be inflicted on groups and individuals in the name of some greater good.

In the Soviet Union, there was little chance of hiding if you were Jewish. It was stamped on your citizenship. And even without examining documents, everyone knew who was "us" and who was "them." In the Soviet Union, we all might have been considered equal "officially," but some were more equal than others, to put it lightly. Jews were frequently beaten, discriminated against, and prohibited from entering certain professions. Within this system, the system that my parents and grandparents grew up in, open conversations were difficult. Say the wrong thing to the wrong person, and you might vanish. It was hard to know who to trust. But all of this hid behind the veneer of an imagined utopia—it was all for the good of the collective. Even though the lineups for food were lengthy and people would spend many months' worth of salary for "black market" items like Levi's, everyone was meant to be happy and . . . equal.

Decades later, when my family began to point out growing similarities between what they'd experienced in the Soviet Union and what they were beginning to see in our adopted country, I was quick to dismiss them. There's no chance of anything like that happening in such a free country, I told them. This is sheer paranoia, I thought.

I was wrong.

Seemingly overnight, certain narratives started to dominate not only public but also, in many cases, private discourse. By now, we are all familiar with these narratives—the ones that see *everything* through the lens of race, gender, and sexuality and that define people accordingly. Like many, I had deep concerns about the way words were being twisted and identities were being weaponized, but I kept my concerns hidden and unexpressed. Working in media and entertainment and living in a fairly progressive city, I certainly wasn't hearing any dissent among my circle of friends and colleagues, and I falsely assumed that only I had questions. I feared that if I spoke up—even if just to investigate rather than confront—I would be ostracized.

I felt depressed. I felt inauthentic. I felt sad. I felt alone.

And then, gradually, I made the decision to speak up a little—at least in person, in private conversations and spaces. Even so, it felt good; finally, I was speaking the truth as I was seeing it—that this burgeoning ideology and many of the policies and proposals and social pressure connected with it were at best illiberal and at worst authoritarian. To my surprise, I discovered that I wasn't alone in my thoughts and reflections. Others were also questioning the dominant narratives and were feeling regret (as well as shame) at their own complacency—but it was done in hushed tones, and no one dared speak up until someone else launched the conversation first. Even when that person turned out to be me, there was a lot I continued to keep private because I remained afraid of being rejected from the tribe. But slowly, inch by inch, I started to gain confidence and find my footing. I was beginning to figure out how to talk to people in ways that might get my points across without antagonizing them. I tried to take them on the journey with me and share my own struggles and ways of questioning things. I was finding more like-minded individuals along the way and was beginning to breathe more freely.

Then everything came to a head.

I had been running a Facebook group that was an offshoot of a bigger "secret" group that was open to women (and later, gender-nonconforming individuals as well) working in media. My particular offshoot, which I—with some help—had launched five years earlier and grown into a group of 30,000+ members, was dedicated to one thing only: connecting women with jobs. Although all of the time I had invested in the group was on a volunteer basis, I was compensated with certain intangible rewards and even public recognition. I was proud to have helped many women find work opportunities, and I even earned a mention in the *New York Times* for launching a mentorship program within the group.

However, the positive and supportive culture and environment that we had worked so hard to cultivate was impossible to maintain. Everything changed when a member of the Facebook group had the "audacity" to post a job opportunity at Fox News. Despite initial interest from a few members, the thread quickly devolved into personal attacks on the person who posted the opening. She was quickly buried in a massive pile-on. For some members of the group, sharing the job opening from such a "fascist, racist regime" was nothing short of an act of "violence."

To me, however, the idea of a mob going after a person for merely sharing a job posting was unsettling. So I, as the founder and administrator of the group, posted a statement asking people to refrain from personal attacks. I also encouraged all members to try to continue to support one another as women in media. The focus of the group is on jobs only—not politics—I reminded them.

In response, the mob turned to me.

The fury and viciousness with which I was attacked stunned me. I was labeled a "white supremacist" who would just as soon let the KKK recruit through the group. I was told that the most reasonable and decent thing for me to do, as a "white woman," was to hand the group over to a woman of color. I was told that my request to keep the group politics free was a "violent act of supremacy and privilege." A group open only to women was inherently political, they argued, and I was thus not allowed to keep it free of politics. In response to this criticism, I suggested that we could solve the problem by opening the group to men—and that's when everything truly imploded. I was harassed, threatened, doxxed, slandered, and libeled. Campaigns were orchestrated to reach out to editors to get me "canceled." For my "sins," I was deserving of no future work. I was told that people had very "long memories" and that I could kiss my career in journalism goodbye. I was sent pictures of mobs with Tiki torches, I was confronted in live online social spaces while speaking on panels, I was slandered and libeled by opportunists with blatant, provable lies, and I was barraged with menacing emails and messages on social media.

But in the midst of all this, as my professional work was being literally and figuratively downvoted by the mob, I was getting another type of message, too. These messages were well-meaning and welcome, but all followed a pattern I came to know well: "I'm so sorry for what's happening to you. I know it's wrong and I wish I could speak up, but I'm absolutely terrified and I feel so ashamed that I'm too scared to stand up for you." Some shared deeply disturbing harassment stories of their own. In a number of cases, this harassment had led them to quit their respective industries. I usually responded by saying how I truly appreciated their message, how it meant so much to me, and how I completely understood their fear and didn't want anyone else to experience the consequences of speaking out. I meant it all, too. Their fear and shame were palpable. I think I probably recognized this feeling so well because I shared it.

But my views on this have since shifted. While I make no judgment on the people who are too afraid to speak out—a decision that's theirs and theirs alone to make—it has become clear to me that this choice to be silent is costing society a great deal. In fact, this is the entire reason for the book you're about to read. My story is just one of many cautionary tales of what happens when we allow the few to speak for the many. In the end, only 2 percent of members left the Facebook group when I refused to step down, and yet the noise they made prior to their departure, in contrast to the silence of the rest of the members, made it impossible to discern the truth of what the majority believed. That was a key insight for me in this episode: when the majority remains silent, a very vocal minority can easily gain complete control of a group even if its views are wildly unpopular. Indeed, this phenomenon not only accounts for many dark moments in history but also explains much about what's happening in our society today.

When I reflect back now, my experience seems so small and insignificant in the grand scheme of things, but at the time—as much as I hesitate using this description—it felt incredibly traumatic. I wasn't sure if I was going to make it out. I didn't want to show emotions; I didn't want anyone to know I was hurting—but I was. The attacks wounded me deeply. I thought better of humans and felt betrayed by my naivety. Every time I thought the experience was behind me, my voice would crackle, and I'd realize that I wasn't quite there yet. I was terrified about the potential loss of my livelihood, my reputation, and my community. But I didn't break. I didn't apologize. And, in some ways, I am now grateful for the experience because it freed me from the remaining shackles I still had on. I became hyperaware of the severity of the problem, and I was finally able to speak honestly and openly—and this time publicly, too.

When I lived in New York, I used to study acting at night in one of the worn-out studios at Carnegie Hall. My teacher, the legendary Robert X Modica, would often say: "When in doubt, repeat or shut up. But when not in doubt, don't repeat, don't shut up: DO." Suddenly I found myself "doing." He'd also say: "It's in the doing that you find out what things mean to you." He was right. What I quickly realized is that in speaking honestly and standing up to the bullies, I was having an effect on others. I knew this because they started to write to me, with pride, to tell me that they had found the courage to speak up about something or to defend someone they saw being bullied—which in turn encouraged others to speak up or step in as well. I had a limited radius, as did others who decided to take a similar approach, but the effects of our actions extended well beyond us, like ripples on a lake. By speaking truth, we were giving others "permission" to do the same. Meanwhile, my own relationships were beginning to feel more honest, too, and I was realizing that far more people shared concerns about the issues we were confronting than not. In fact, we were collectively realizing that our views aligned because we were finally saying what we really thought, out loud, for the first time.

Yet, in truth, not all outcomes from my experience have been positive. Freeing my voice has led to some negative results, too. I've certainly lost some people I thought were friends (though, fortunately, none of my close ones). Some even proved themselves willing to listen to lies without ever verifying whether they were true with me. I'm constantly nervous about whether anyone I meet knows about my "back story." (I didn't used to have one.) When a former client passed on me for a position I would have normally been a shoo-in for, I had no way of knowing whether this was a result of those warned-about "long memories." There's an anxiety that never quite leaves me, as much as I try to be dismissive of it. I don't trust people as easily anymore. And this mindset can feel enormously lonely sometimes—especially as someone who didn't have a large group of people rallying behind me to begin with.

When I wrote the op-ed about my experience for *Newsweek*, I was certain that I was about to blow up my life—and most definitely my career. I thought that the mob would return, with more torches this time. My family, concerned, initially pleaded with me not to publish it. "You're going to destroy your career and life, and for what? You're not going to make any difference." That might have been the way to survive in the Soviet Union—where the situation was rather hopeless, but I knew it was the right thing to do in our current moment. I didn't know who I'd be if I didn't try to make some difference, to at least try and stand up. Even though I may not reach millions of people on my own, I had a circle of people I could connect with—and they each had their own circles. I wanted to ensure that others knew they were not alone, and I wanted to empower them to speak.

But I also knew I didn't have all the answers—and everyone faces their own unique set of challenges, some far more complex and fraught than my own, which is, ultimately, why I kept "going." Just as others had reached out to me upon hearing about my story, I started reaching out to others who had faced the cancellation mob. I wanted to see what they had, in retrospect, learned from their experiences. What had they done right—and wrong. After two years of research and writing, I found there are clear lessons to be found in the experiences of others—lessons that I wish I had known earlier in my journey. I still don't have all the answers, but I believe even more strongly today that now, more than ever, it's time for the reasonable majority to free their voices and speak out for tolerance and freedom of thought. The experiences and lessons shared in this book will help us all do this. We don't have to agree about everything all the time, but we should be able to have conversations about everything all the time. Silencing culture is a dangerous and illiberal phenomenon that has an easy solution. All that's required is that we speak up.

So let's push back and find our voices—together.

## Notes

My *Newsweek* article provides more details on my experience with the Facebook group. See Katherine Brodsky, "The Rise of Righteous Online Bullies," *Newsweek*, May 24, 2021, www.newsweek.com/rise-righteous-online-bullies-opinion-1593704.

# NO APOLOGIES

# Introduction: The Silenced Majority

For most of us, the loss of one's voice usually happens gradually. First, it's a small adjustment to the words that you use. "Blind" becomes "visually impaired," "fat" is discarded for "overweight," "homeless" is replaced with "unhoused," and "idiotic" is replaced with "uninformed." Some academics even suggest words like "American," "prisoner," and "victim" should be off-limits due to the harm they believe the words to cause and the messages they perceive them to convey. Oh, and you don't talk about the "black sheep" of the family anymore—you talk about the "outcast" member of the family. And you no longer "take a shot at" something—rather, you "give a go at" it instead. You go along with many of these alternative words and phrases to be polite. You apologize for your errors.

Soon, other seemingly harmless requests and rules are introduced. You are told not to wear a certain dress or hairstyle from another culture because to do so is "cultural appropriation." You are told the word "man" includes everyone who self-identifies as one. You are told that only white people can be racist. And you are told you must believe all women, and you must never question the "lived experience" of anyone from an underrepresented minority. And you hesitantly go along with all this, too, even if all these new rules don't all necessarily make sense to you. After all, everyone else is going along, and you don't want to be an outlier within your own social circle. Before long, you realize that you're better off not expressing any thoughts, ideas, or questions—lest you offend anyone. Of course, you don't intend to offend, but it's hard to tell what might offend any given person. It is in the eye of the beholder. So, you stop talking altogether or stick to the weather because you don't want to be disagreeable or cause a fight, and you certainly don't want to be ostracized or destroy a career you've spent a lifetime building. Besides, you've got a family to feed.

That's how regular people get silenced—little by little each day as their vocabularies and beliefs are bounded by an ever-shrinking box. Gradually. Like a frog in boiling water, you barely realize what's happening until it's too late; the temperature just keeps slowly creeping up. Boxed in that silence, you begin to lose yourself. And it is in that mass silence that we, as a society, lose our ability to have meaningful, nuanced discourse and give up our voices to those who crave the power to control others. That's the price we pay. But our coffers are starting to come up empty. When we see so many clamoring to denounce others over highly subjective perceptions of objectionable behavior or speech, anyone can find themselves as a target. And as we've been witnessing, it doesn't take much for the accusations to fly fast and loose. All it takes is expressing a different opinion on a social or political issue, or asking the wrong question—or even believing in an idea or principle that was widely shared by the chattering class just a few short years ago but that today is considered forbidden in polite society. It can even be as small a slight as accidentally mispronouncing someone's name.

For individuals, the stakes are high. Livelihoods, reputations, careers, social standing—all can disappear in the blink of an eye. As we've all too tragically seen, some never recover—even if they first put up a brave fight. For society, the stakes are no less high. As we as a society grow increasingly intolerant, we undermine the very ideals of a democratic society from within, edging ever closer to authoritarianism. A July 2023 survey from the University of Chicago's Project on Security and Threats found that 17 percent of American adults—an estimated 44 million people—agree with the following statement: "Use of force is justified to ensure members of Congress and other government officials do the right thing." Democrats (16 percent) and Republicans (18 percent) are almost even in this belief. We can only guess what "the right thing" might be. Given the oversized impact the zealous few can have on the political and cultural landscape, these numbers are sobering, if not chilling. The one promising finding in the survey is that 77 percent of the American public opposes political violence and wants bipartisan solutions to it, but this opposition will be toothless and ineffectual if this majority does not raise its voice—both in words and through action. While the *Washington Post* might be correct in noting that "Democracy Dies in Darkness," it also dies in silence.

Across the West, attempts are being made to soften the sometimes clanky but always necessary sounds of the democratic engine—freedom of speech and freedom of expression. In the United Kingdom, police have been tracking and recording "non-crime hate incidents" and logging them with no investigation or due process, and the passage of the Online Safety Bill will give the government the power to censor and shut down online content. Under Ireland's "draconian" Criminal Justice (Incitement to Violence or Hatred and Hate Offences) Bill, citizens might soon be charged with a crime if they say or write something that someone from a protected class finds hateful or offensive. If a single person from such a class finds your words hateful, then based on the bill's logic, your words are not only hateful but also criminal.

In Canada, Bill C-11, known as the Online Streaming Act, which was first proposed in 2020 and received royal assent in 2023, allows the government the power to regulate online speech and even shut down the social media and streaming accounts of Canadians. Meanwhile, the Online Harms Bill, first tabled in 2021 as Bill C-36 and since rebranded as the Online Safety Bill, would have those who engage in hate online, be it via social media or public comments on news articles, face criminal charges. While most of us are not likely to consider "hate speech" as a form of expression that adds value to our lives, it is, in fact, protected by section 2(b) of the *Charter of Rights and Freedoms*, which guarantees individuals' freedom of expression. What's particularly worrisome about the proposed bill is the interpretation of "hatred," which the bill defines as "the emotion that involves detestation or vilification and that is stronger than dislike or disdain." In response, the Canadian Constitution Foundation (CCF) issued a statement that argues that the bill would be an infringement on free expression—namely, that the proposed definition of hate speech is "a vague and subjective standard." It also expressed concern that the bill would prevent Canadians from "debating unsettled subjects."

In the United Kingdom, the penalties for hate speech can include fines, imprisonment, or both—including for posts on social media. Although newer numbers are hard to come by, a total of 2,500 people were arrested between 2011 and 2016 in London alone for allegedly sending "offensive" messages via social media under the country's 2003 Communications Act and legislation pertaining to public order, with police arresting nine people per day across the United Kingdom by the end of this five-year span, representing an increase of 50 percent in two years. As one example illustrating the type of legal overreach that has been occurring, Chelsea Russell, a teenager in Liverpool, was charged with a "hate crime" after a screenshot was anonymously sent to police of her quoting lyrics from Snap Dogg's "I'm Trippin," which included the N-word, on her Instagram account. She had posted the lyrics as a tribute to a friend who had died in a car accident, as it was his favorite song. Although the case against her was later overturned, she was initially given an eight-week community service order and curfew and was ordered to pay fines. In recent years, individuals have been fined or arrested for such minor offenses as sharing a meme.

In the United States, things are slightly better, thanks to the strong free speech protections enshrined in the First Amendment, but even there, a national debate on where the limitations of acceptable speech should be drawn is ongoing. While much of the debate continues to revolve around speech deemed to be blasphemous, hateful, discriminatory, or deceitful, a new front has opened up in recent years: speech charged with promoting "disinformation" or "misinformation" or threatening national security. The potential implementation of the Restrict Act, for example, which currently has bipartisan support, would give the federal government the ability to regulate and even ban technology owned in whole or part by foreign adversaries. As many note, this far-reaching bill could lead to bans on applications like TikTok and restrictions on VPNs (virtual private networks) and thus threaten a free and open Internet in the name of protecting the United States and its citizens. Toward this end, the Biden administration also launched—and ultimately rescinded—a "disinformation governance board," which had been tasked with helping the Department of Homeland Security "address the disinformation threat streams that can undermine the security of our homeland," but which critics compared to Orwell's Ministry of Truth. As the legal scholar Jonathan Turley aptly noted, "If the government can define what is a lie, it can define what is the truth."

In today's world, where long-established boundaries between public and private institutions have become increasingly blurred, governments need not even take any direct legislative action to quell speech when they have willing accomplices. Tech companies everywhere, for example, have taken their own steps to curb online speech, as revealed in the Twitter Files, in which the company's new CEO, Elon Musk, provided select journalists with access to internal Twitter documents that showed Twitter (now known as X) had an established pattern of submitting to takedown requests from U.S. officials, and by Mark Zuckerberg, who has admitted that Facebook censored truthful stories about Hunter Biden based on direct misinformation warnings by the FBI in the lead up to the 2020 U.S. presidential elections. YouTube, meanwhile, has long had what writer Helen Lewis refers to as a "forest of invisible trip wires" and has a history of aggressively cracking down on speech that conflicts with government narratives. These examples of censorship amount to, in the words of Frederick Douglass, a "double wrong"—a violation of not only the rights of the speaker but also the hearer.

Universities, meanwhile, have been quick to jump on the bandwagon, especially when there's government funding available for studies on how to best manage and improve online censorship. "Disinformation studies" has become a fast-growing field, emerging in the wake of Brexit and the election of Donald Trump, that is taken seriously at top academic institutions. Harvard University's Kennedy School, for example, publishes a journal titled *HKS Misinformation Review*. A 2023 report in that journal argued "mis- and disinformation studies are too big to fail." The Foundation for Freedom Online has documented how, in the first two years of the Biden administration alone, more than forty colleges and universities received sixty-four government "mis/disinformation" grants from the National Science Foundation. It notes, "This incredible range of recipients covers every level of the country's higher education institutions, both regionally and in terms of prestige."

At the same time, many universities have begun making hiring decisions and promotions based on the diversity, equity, and inclusion (DEI) statements of candidates, a practice that, on its face, amounts to a political litmus test. This practice not only overlooks real diversity but also falls afoul of a key tenet of free expression: a free society, by definition, requires not only free speech but also freedom from compelled speech. In the wake of the U.S. Supreme Court's ruling against affirmative action in college admissions, DEI initiatives that impinge on the rights of individuals appear to be the next major legal battle. Indeed, a spate of lawsuits has already been launched, accusing not just universities but also corporations, hospitals, and nonprofit organizations of discrimination in the name of diversity, inclusion, and equity.

Yet, in many cases, governments and their corporate and university allies are not even the loudest and most enthusiastic censors. The role of cheerleader goes to our fellow citizens—or, for lack of a better pronoun, us. In the United States, for example, more than half of those surveyed (55 percent) in 2023 by the Pew Research Center think the U.S. government should "restrict false information online." When broken down along partisan lines, 71 percent of Democrats and Democrat leaners supported this idea, while 59 percent of Republicans and Republican leaners were against it. This is a stunning departure from recent decades when the Democrats were seen as the party of free speech. Indeed, this shift is quite recent. In 2018, for example, only 40 percent of Democrats and Democrat leaners supported this idea—roughly even with Republicans and Republican leaners (37 percent). When looking specifically at steps technology companies should take, a large majority of Democrats and Democratic leaners (81 percent) today would like to see technology companies restrict "false information online," while about half of Republicans and Republican leaners (48 percent) would like to see the same. Meanwhile, 48 percent of U.S. adults are in favor of the government taking steps to restrict false information—even if that meant restricting their ability to access and publish some content. In short, nearly half of the country is willing to give up their fundamental rights and allow the government and big tech corporations to restrict both our freedom to share information and our freedom to access it.

When looking specifically at younger generations—students and young adults who have grown up with the idea that speech itself can be a form of violence—the percentage would likely be even higher. Indeed, attitudes toward free speech seem to be shifting dramatically in the wrong direction among high school and college students. According to Pew Research, 62 percent of U.S. teens (ages 13 to 17) say that they value others being able to feel welcome and safe online over individuals being able to speak their minds freely. As polls show, this younger cohort sees speech as something dangerous that must be policed and punished, including with actual violence. In a 2022 survey conducted by the Buckley Institute at Yale University, for example, 41 percent of college students said they were in favor of using violence to stop "hateful" speech, a rise of 5 percent from 2021, and nearly half (48 percent) agreed that sometimes speech can be so offensive that it merits the death penalty. In a 2023 survey from the Institute for Global Innovation and Growth at North Dakota State University, an alarming 76 percent of students said that they would report a professor for saying something offensive, with self-identified liberal students roughly 50 percent more likely to report one than a self-identified conservative student.

These findings are consistent with any number of other surveys and studies. For example, the Foundation for Individual Rights and Expression (FIRE) conducted the largest survey of college free speech ever in 2022–23. It found that 40 percent of students are uncomfortable disagreeing with a professor—whether in public or in a written assignment. Notably, 42 percent of conservative students "often" feel uncomfortable speaking freely, while only 13 percent of liberal students report the same. Meanwhile, 59 to 73 percent of those surveyed were opposed to allowing controversial conservative speakers on campus, depending on the topic and speaker, but only 24 to 41 percent of those surveyed were opposed to controversial liberal speakers. These same attitudes can be found in graduate and professional schools as well.

Consider the reception given to Kyle Duncan, a conservative federal judge whose prepared talk at an event hosted by Stanford Law School's Federalist Society chapter was thwarted by dozens of disorderly law students. Rather than removing the disruptive protestors, Tirien Steinbach, the school's associate dean for diversity, equity, and inclusion, approached the podium to side with the students and give her seal of approval to their heckler's veto. The university eventually apologized to the judge, but after the event, many questioned how these future lawyers could have such disregard for fundamental principles like free speech and "the essential skill of citizenship: knowing how to agree to disagree with one another." Indeed, the stifling of free speech is a growing concern in college campuses across North America, with celebrated schools like Stanford, Georgetown, and Yale making FIRE's "10 Worst Colleges for Free Speech" list in 2022.

The same sort of thing regularly happens in the United Kingdom and Canada as well. At the University of British Columbia, for example, the university's Free Speech Club has been known for bringing in speakers like Jordan B. Peterson, Ben Shapiro, and Stephen Hicks—not always to all the student body's delight. But when Andy Ngo, editor-at-large of *The Post Millennial*, was scheduled to give a talk titled "Understanding Antifa (Anti-fascist) Violence," the university shut down the event out of safety and security concerns. As a result, the school's Free Speech Club, alongside the Justice Centre for Constitutional Freedoms (JCCF), filed a lawsuit against the university. This is not a one-off thing. Events of this nature are often canceled in advance due to either alleged or real security concerns. In 2019, for example, Simon Fraser University had an event organized by a faculty member canceled and relocated for security reasons by its sponsor. The event, called "How Media Bias Shapes the Gender Debate," drew criticism for featuring writer Meghan Murphy, who at the time was banned on Twitter for referring to a trans woman as "him."

This type of threat-based activism is not wielded only against invited speakers but also extends to faculty already on campus. FIRE's Scholars Under Fire Database tracks "targeting incidents" among faculty and other scholars on campus. In 2021, it documented 111 scholars who had been subject to a targeting incident, defined as "a campus controversy involving efforts to investigate, penalize, or otherwise *professionally* sanction a scholar for engaging in constitutionally protected forms of speech," usually for expressing a personal view or opinion on a controversial social issue. Over one-third of targeting incidents occurred because of a scholar's scientific inquiry or teaching practices. More than 60 percent of targeting incidents resulted in some form of sanction being leveled against the scholar. In 2015, only 30 such incidents were documented.

Of course, this type of "targeting" is a serious issue outside of academia as well, though records are tougher to establish and maintain. In many U.S. states and Canadian provinces, employees can be terminated at will and without cause, often without notice. This means that it can be impossible to even officially ascertain if a termination is due to off-hours speech, performance, or company downsizing. Thus, even if an employee has a strong suspicion that their dismissal is related to something they said on social media or the message on the bumper sticker on their car, they are left with no mechanism to dispute this.

Some people argue that this is nothing but accountability culture and, thus, these individuals deserve the consequences of the words they chose. Indeed, accountability is important in a healthy, functioning society. It means that we hold people responsible for their actions and, ideally, give them an opportunity to make things right—or at least make it so that they can't cause further harm. But too often, we've moved the line far past accountability. The silencing culture that has been festering is purely punitive in nature and offers no chance for dialogue or discussion, let alone reconciliation or redemption. It lacks any form of due process and offers swift judgment with little chance of appeal. It is also based on arbitrary rules and subjective language. In most cases, the punishment is so disproportionate and extreme that it does not fit the presumed "crime." Indeed, those who lose their jobs or reputations have often committed no actual crime except to think about the world a bit differently or be unfamiliar with the shibboleths of the day. And the jury, judge, and executioner are the mob. But the mob almost never represents the popular or majority view; rather, it gives the impression of enjoying universal support and backing by being loud and aggressive. After all, it need only make examples of the few to change the language and behavior of the many and exert control. Ultimately, the silent majority is scared to speak up, stand up, or object.

But not everyone who has been mobbed submits or stays silent, no matter how hard the bullies try to shut them up. For those who have managed to maintain or even free their voices, what is it about them that has allowed them to do so? What did they go through as a result? What does their experience say about the society that we've become? And, most importantly, how do we reverse this oppressive trend? The fear of speaking up is nothing new. Not all German citizens reported their Jewish neighbors to the Gestapo, but few spoke out as Jews were systemically stripped of their rights and ultimately sent to camps to be exterminated. Likewise, during China's Cultural Revolution, children were encouraged to denounce their parents, classmates, and each other. There was an obvious chill, and no one knew whom to trust. Similarly, in Russia, it was not unusual for a black car to show up in the middle of the night to take your neighbor away. Political dissidents were sent away to work camps or Gulags. No one knew whom to trust with the truth. Currently, in North Korea, not only are citizens afraid of punishment by death for saying the wrong thing, but they are also taught what to say and whom to praise. We might believe that this is far from our own reality and that we are immune, but the truth is that these things don't happen overnight. As anyone who has even completed a cursory study of history knows, the cliché phrase "history repeats itself" is undisputedly true—particularly if we fail to learn from it. Staying silent always ends up being far more dangerous than speaking up. We are never as far away from totalitarianism or authoritarianism as we think. All it takes is for enough people to say . . . nothing.

Saying nothing is often the easy way out. A modern version of the fight or flight response. Just as humans have a tendency to retreat to silence as an individual survival mechanism, the urge to silence also exists in everyone. The instinct to want to censor that with which we disagree exists across politics and culture. Each group feels like it is uniquely justified in its silencing efforts. Consider the calls to fire teachers who speak about certain subjects in the classroom or the banning of books. Just as one side believes that it is justified in silencing, so does the other. On balance, though, in today's world, the institutions that we rely upon

—schools, media, government, and corporations—have been "captured" by the intolerant far left more than the intolerant right. For now. As such, the battlelines over free speech—its definition, boundaries, and contours—are often more about power than principle. At any moment, the roles can easily be reversed—just as core philosophical or ideological commitments have been reversed over time. Indeed, one of the most stunning sociopolitical developments of the past decade is how the very principle of free speech went from being long associated with the political left to being suddenly associated with the political right—especially in the North American context. But despite many conservatives turning into adamant supporters of the First Amendment, things can reverse course just as quickly. On March 24, 2023, FIRE sued West Texas A&M University President Walter Wendler for violating the First Amendment right of college students to hold a charity drag show on campus. The event was meant to raise money for suicide prevention among LGBTQ+ youth. (FIRE, which is a nonpartisan organization, also recently sued a Michigan school district for ordering students to remove "Let's Go Brandon" sweatshirts). The judge presiding on the case ultimately ruled that the student fundraiser featuring drag performers was not protected speech. There's no shortage of such stories from both spectrums, with more occurring every week. The cure to this is a renewed commitment to free speech as the foundational element of our politics and society. As often stated, championing free speech for those with views you like is easy; free speech means nothing if it's not also granted to those with views you don't like—or even abhor.

To make my own experiences and allegiances clear, in my journey to free my voice, I have increasingly found myself as the "token liberal" in conservative-dominated spaces and have thus been attacked by both the left and the right—often through what I euphemistically refer to as "fan mail." The "fan mail" I receive from the intolerant left is generally worded better than the missives from the intolerant right, but the words tend to have more venom to them and present a more active threat than those coming from the right. Ultimately, I perceive them as being more dangerous for a simple reason: they have power behind them. The "fan" could actually harm me. The "fan" could destroy my reputation and livelihood. The venom comes with the real possibility of widespread media coverage and mass mobilization of a mob that enjoys tremendous cultural, social, and political power. On the other hand, the "fan mail" I receive from the intolerant right tends to be more vulgar but has less bite. The words are angry yet come off as desperate—because, inevitably, the writer behind them is institutionally powerless. These messages never feel like a real threat. Would it be different if power was distributed differently? Absolutely. I see that very clearly from the conversations I've observed or been party to.

The intolerant left likes to weaponize accusations of racism, bigotry, sexism, transphobia, and white supremacy against anyone who disagrees or even questions. Although these powerful terms are the ones that trigger investigations, firings, and media coverage, they are devalued with each instance of misuse. Meanwhile, the intolerant right relies on its own kinds of tropes and likes to denounce anyone who disagrees with them as libtards, snowflakes, purple-haired people, tankies, or groomers. None of these are particularly useful for starting discourse, but all are certainly effective at ending discussion and silencing dialogue. The silliness of these aspersions aside, let's be clear: the intolerant right is no less of an "enemy" to free speech and unity than the intolerant left.

The misuse of words in the service of gaining some individual or collective advantage relies on what I call "word misappropriation," a phenomenon that occurs when a group of people pillages a particular word or term, declares its own definition of it, and then insists that the rest of us accept that very definition and all the beliefs that follow. When robbed of their true meaning and deployed in this fashion, the words, at best, do little more than cause confusion. At worst, they serve as weapons intended to destroy those at which they are directed. In a society where we can't even agree on the definitions of words, how can we begin to discuss the concepts that they represent? Not everything is racist, sexist, transphobic, fascistic, white supremacist, etc., nor is everyone a groomer, tankie, snowflake, Nazi, etc. As an eternal optimist, I think it's important to note that there are people from all spectrums who believe in defending each other's speech and engaging with respect, regardless of whether they agree or disagree. This is what we should foster. A culture of tolerance. A culture that does not condone the silencing of others, whether through legal means, social levers, or weaponized language.

Although the question of how and why we got here is a supremely important one, that is not the focus of this book, which has a more specific focus and intent: encouraging individuals to free their voices and identifying lessons for doing so. For those of us who have yet to find or free our voice—for those in the silent majority—it features select stories of individuals who have been the target of the outrage mob, often for speaking out about a subject important to them. In all cases, attempts were made to silence these individuals, but all either continue to speak out—or have finally begun to use their voices to speak out—not without further consequences. While the process of being silenced is often gradual for the general public, for the individuals featured in this book, the repercussions from saying the wrong thing, whether intentionally or by accident, were often sudden—even immediate. Some have managed to stay strong and fight back despite strong opposition, while others haven't fared as well.

The stories in this book are told from the perspective of those interviewed and are, for the most part, expressed in their own words as relayed to me. The intention of the book, therefore, is to shed light on what silencing looks and feels like in practice. It is also intended to identify lessons for others who might experience the same—or who simply want to learn to free their own voice. Here, I offer two important things to keep in mind as you read: First, you will likely encounter ideas and opinions in this book with which you strongly disagree. After all, many of the people I interviewed for this book are known for promoting and advancing ideas that have a track record of drawing intense scrutiny and attention. My intent is not to litigate or judge the merits of their specific ideas, nor do I mean to endorse or discredit any of them. Rather, my intent is to give them a chance to tell their stories, to provide some context about their experiences, to reflect on what they've done right and wrong, and to provide lessons for others who may be fearful of speaking out or who may already be targeted by the bullying mob. Second, for each story that's included in this book, there are countless others that have not yet been shared, including from voices that have been effectively extinguished—from individuals whose careers and lives have been completely destroyed. Important lessons can undoubtedly be gleaned from those stories as well.

In a matter of years, we've become terrified as a society of voicing disagreements or even asking the kinds of questions that are essential if we want to keep our society in check. Truly open conversations are crucial because they allow for the kind of push and pull that allows us to test our own beliefs about the world. This is true whether we're talking about public, economic, educational, or scientific policy. When it comes to such matters, our perception of consensus is also important to keep in mind. Where does consensus come from? More often than not, our impression is formed by the media, but what is communicated by media is dependent on many factors. For example, many studies are backed by corporate interests, and journals are edited and managed by individuals with their own biases and motivations. Connections matter, too. And when it comes to reporting on the data, few journalists actually take the time to read all the relevant research, and fewer still have the expertise to understand and evaluate it. More often than not, they are reporting on a summary that's being sent to them and are being connected to pre-approved experts to provide commentary. The story, if framed properly, then travels around from publication to publication—and if that happens enough, in the public consciousness, the narrative becomes akin to indisputable fact. In this process, the truth can be lost.

When it comes to science specifically, there is a tendency to trust scientific consensus. There's a sense that if enough experts in the field agree, then a particular scientific hypothesis must be correct. Oftentimes—particularly if the hypothesis has been rigorously tested—that assumption is correct. But not always. Despite all the rallying cries to "believe science," it is not a religion to be believed or worshipped. It is a methodological process by which scientists intellectually, practically, and experimentally investigate, reason about, and record the world around us to try and understand it the best we can using evidence, data, and observation. And in order for it to properly work, it must be free of bias, political interference, and outside pressure. Despite claims to the contrary, science is never settled. After all, have we not, time and time again, shifted our understanding of the world based on new discoveries? Have scientific ideas never been proven wrong? We are always limited by the information that's available to us at any given time. With new evidence, our understanding shifts. That's how science works.

Whether in the sciences or any other field of human endeavor, we cannot make our own arguments stronger or change our views based on better information that's presented to us unless we allow challenges to our ideas and beliefs. But none of this can happen under duress. We can't effectively pursue truth or improve systems or question the mainstream consensus if we are being labeled things we are not, if we are worried about being libeled, slandered, or harassed, or if we fear losing our jobs or being ousted from our communities, merely for daring to think about the world a little differently. But we live in a time where too many people are desperately afraid of speaking up or standing up for each other—even our own friends. In many cases, we're letting a loud and intimidating yet often small group of people silence us. The mob isn't demanding that we face consequences for poor behavior but rather asserting that anyone who goes against their particular narrative or ideology can and should be persecuted. Through the stories in this book, I hope to give the reader a sense of what the problem is and ideas about how we can each push back. *Why do our voices matter, and what keeps someone from using theirs? What makes some people more likely to speak out than others, and how can we empower the silent majority to speak up?*

Many of the individuals featured in this book will be familiar to you; others will not be. Some of these stories you may already know—or at least think you know. Although we all need to learn to speak up, like those on the following pages have, it's important to remember that in this era of heightened public scrutiny, not everyone comes out on top—even if a number of people who have been mobbed have managed to find their way in some form or another. Discussion of controversial topics and heterodoxy always comes with a warning tag. Buyer beware: your career and professional standing may be jeopardized. You may no longer be able to make a living. And if the cost is not financial, then it will certainly be social. The business of expressing your opinions is a serious one and may profoundly change the trajectory of your life, often for the better but sometimes for the worse. Results may vary. Be prepared.

Freeing your voice often comes with a price, just as staying silent does—but as the following stories reveal, speaking unapologetically also offers immense rewards. Staying silent offers none.

## Notes

There have been multiple stories regarding "harmful language." For one such story, see Elizabeth Redden, "Amid Backlash, Stanford Removes 'Harmful Language' List," *Inside Higher Ed*, January 11, 2023, www.insidehighered.com/news/2023/01/11/amid-backlash-stanford-re-moves-harmful-language-list#:~:text=The%20Elimination%20of%20Harmful%20Language,we%20missed%20the%20intended%20mark.

Attacks on free speech in the form of bullying have real-world effects, causing harm both to society and to individuals. One of the first contemporary books to call attention to this issue was Jonathan Rauch's *Kindly*

*Inquisitors: The New Attacks on Free Thought,* expanded ed. (University of Chicago Press, 2013), originally published in 1993, and one of the most recent is *The Canceling of the American Mind: Cancel Culture Undermines Trust and Threatens Us All—But There Is a Solution,* by Greg Lukianoff and Rikki Schlott (Simon and Schuster, 2023).

For a specific instance of ideological bullying that led to suicide, see "RIP, Richard Bilkszto, a Toronto Educator Who Stood up to Woke Bullying—and Paid the Price," *Quillette,* July 21, 2023, quillette.com/2023/07/21/rip-richard-bilkszto.

For the University of Chicago survey, see Robert A. Pape, "July 2023 Survey Report: Tracking Deep Distrust of Democratic Institutions, Conspiracy Beliefs, and Support for Political Violence Among Americans." CPOST Chicago Project on Security and Terrorism, July 10, 2023, cpost.uchicago.edu/publications/july_2023_survey_report_tracking_deep_distrust_of_democratic_institutions_conspiracy_beliefs_and_support_for_political_violenc_among_americans.

For the United Kingdom's Online Safety Bill and the recording and retention of personal data, see "Online Safety Bill: Progress of the Bill," House of Commons Library, October 6, 2023, commonslibrary.parliament.uk/research-briefings/cbp-9579; "Non-Crime Hate Incidents: Code of Practice on the Recording and Retention of Personal Data (accessible)—GOV.UK." GOV.UK, June 3, 2023, www.gov.uk/government/publications/non-crime-hate-incidents-code-of-practice/non-crime-hate-incidents-code-of-practice-on-the-recording-and-retention-of-personal-data-accessible; and "UK Police's Speech-Chilling Practice of Tracking 'Non-Crime Hate Incidents,'" Foundation for Individual Rights in Education (FIRE), September 22, 2023, www.thefire.org/news/uk-polices-speech-chilling-practice-tracking-non-crime-hate-incidents.

For more on Ireland's Criminal Justice (Incitement to Violence or Hatred and Hate Offences) Bill, see "Incitement to Hatred and Hate Crime Bill 2022." Oireachtas, 2022, www.oireachtas.ie/en/bills/bill/2022/105; and Brendan O'Neill, "Ireland's Deeply Sinister Hate Crime Bill," *Spec-*

*tator*, September 21, 2023, www.spectator.co.uk/article/irelands-deeply-sinister-hate-crime-bill.

For more on Canada's effort to expand government regulation of online and hate speech, see Jamil Jivani, "Trudeau Is Crushing Free Speech in Canada. Let It Be a Warning to the US," *Newsweek*, March 14, 2023, www.newsweek.com/trudeau-crushing-free-speech-canada-let-it-warning-us-opinion-1787480; and Parliament of Canada, "An Act to Amend the Criminal Code (Hate Propaganda, Hate Crimes and Hate Speech)." Parliament of Canada, June 23, 2021, www.parl.ca/DocumentViewer/en/43-2/bill/C-36/first-reading. For the Canadian Constitution Foundation's June 23, 2021, statement on the Online Harms Bill, theccf.ca/canadian-constitution-foundation-statement-on-online-harms-bill.

The arrests over social media posts in the United Kingdom have received high-profile coverage. See, for example, Sadie Levy Gale, "Arrests for Offensive Facebook Posts Are Increasing in London," *Independent*, September 27, 2023, www.independent.co.uk/news/uk/arrests-for-offensive-facebook-and-twitter-posts-soar-in-london-a7064246.html; and Charlie Parker, "Police Arresting Nine People per Day in Fight against Web Trolls," *Times*, October 12, 2017, www.thetimes.co.uk/article/police-arresting-nine-people-a-day-in-fight-against-web-trolls-b8nkpgp2d; BBC News. "Woman Guilty of 'Racist' Snap Dogg Rap Lyric Instagram Post," BBC News, September 23, 2023, www.bbc.com/news/uk-england-merseyside-43816921; and "I Was Arrested over a Meme' Britain's Free Speech Crisis Explained." YouTube, video uploaded by the *Telegraph* on September 1, 2022, www.youtube.com/watch?v=YyMGO2MO6GU.

Turley's quote comes from Jonathan Turley, "The Death of Free Speech," *Jonathan Turley's Blog*, October 14, 2012, jonathanturley.org/2012/10/14/the-death-of-free-speech.

Lewis's comments on YouTube come from Helen Lewis, "What You Can't Say on YouTube," *Atlantic*, September 20, 2023, www.theatlantic.com/ideas/archive/2023/03/youtube-content-moderation-rules/673322.

For more on "disinformation studies" and the U.S. government's support for it, see Chico Q. Camargo and Felix M. Simon, "Mis- and Disinformation Studies Are Too Big to Fail: Six Suggestions for the Field's Future," *HKS Misinformation Review*, September 22, 2022, misinforeview.hks.harvard.edu/article/mis-and-disinformation-studies-are-too-big-to-fail-six-suggestions-for-the-fields-future; and Mike Benz, "Censorship's Permanent Home In Academia: Harvard Journal Bragged 'Mis/Disinfo Studies' Is 'Too Big to Fail,'" Foundation for Freedom Online, May 30, 2023, foundationforfreedomonline.com/harvard-too-big-to-fail.

For more on how DEI statements, ideological tests, and "cancel culture" are in conflict with the principle of free speech, see Editorial Board. "'Antiracists' vs. Academic Freedom," *Wall Street Journal*, September 29, 2023, www.wsj.com/articles/daymon-johnson-lawsuit-california-community-colleges-bakersfield-deia-faculty-education-7fc2763e; Yannick Thoraval, "I'm a University Lecturer and Wokeism Is Stifling Free Debate in My Classroom," *Sydney Morning Herald*, March 16, 2023, www.smh.com.au/education/i-m-a-university-lecturer-and-wokeism-is-stifling-free-debate-in-my-classroom-20230316-p5csor.html; Editorial Board, "America Has a Free Speech Problem," *New York Times*, March 18, 2022, www.nytimes.com/2022/03/18/opinion/cancel-culture-free-speech-poll.html; Kelley Bregenzer, "Victory: FIRE Forces Berkeley to Turn over Records Related to DEI Hiring Policy after Two-Year Delay," FIRE, June 14, 2023, www.thefire.org/news/victory-fire-forces-berkeley-turn-over-records-related-dei-hiring-policy-after-two-year-delay; and Zaid Jilani, "The Diversity Trap," *Tablet Magazine*, June 29, 2020, www.tabletmag.com/sections/news/articles/the-diversity-trap-jilani.

For the various free-speech surveys and commentary on them, see "More Americans Now Say Government Should Take Steps to Restrict False Information Online Than in 2018," Pew Research Center, August 18, 2021, www.pewresearch.org/short-reads/2021/08/18/more-americans-now-say-government-should-take-steps-to-restrict-false-information-online-than-in-2018; "Buckley Program Releases Eighth Annual College Student Survey." Buckley Institute, October 25, 2022, buckleyinstitute.com/buckley-program-releases-eighth-annual-college-student-survey; Jonathan Turkey, "Pew: Seventy Percent of Democrats and Democratic-Leaning Independents Support Speech Limits," *Jonathan Turley's Blog*, July 27, 2023, jonathan-turley.org/2023/07/27/pew-seventy-percent-of-democrats-and-demo-cratic-leaning-independents-support-speech-limits; and "Students Likely to Report Instructors for Offensive Comments," *Inside Higher Ed*, July 21, 2023, www.insidehighered.com/news/students/free-speech/2023/07/21/students-likely-report-instructors-offensive-comments.

For more on the issue of the "heckler's veto" and the canceling of speaking events on campus, see Karen Sloan Nate Raymond, "Stanford Law Official Who Admonished Judge During Speech Is on Leave, Dean Says," Reuters, March 22, 2023, www.reuters.com/legal/legalindustry/stanford-law-official-who-admonished-judge-during-speech-is-leave-dean-says-2023-03-22; James Ho and Elizabeth Branch, "Stop the Chaos: Law Schools Need to Crack Down on Student Disrupters Now," *National Review*, March 15, 2023, www.nationalreview.com/2023/03/stop-the-chaos-law-schools-need-to-crack-down-on-student-disrupters-now; Jennifer Saltman, "UBC Event Cancelled, Debate Continues about Free Expression on Campus, *Vancouver Sun*, January 2, 2020, vancouversun.com/news/local-news/ubc-event-cancelled-debate-continues-about-free-expression-on-campus ; Jerry Coyne, January 6, 2020, "UBC Cancels Free Speech Event on Grounds of 'risk,'" *Why Evolution Is True*, whyevolutionistrue.com/2020/01/06/ubc-cancels-free-speech-event-on-grounds-of-risk.

For FIRE's list, see "10 Worst Colleges for Free Speech: 2022" FIRE, February 22, 2022, www.thefire.org/news/10-worst-colleges-free-speech-2022. It has released a "top ten" list every year since 2011. For the annual lists, www.thefire.org/research-learn/worst-colleges-free-speech.

For more on FIRE's "Scholars Under Fire" report, see www.thefire.org/research-learn/scholars-under-fire-2021-year-review#:~:text=In%20the%20database%2C%20we%20include,in%20some%20form%20of%20sanction; and *Inside Higher Ed*, "Tracking Attacks

on Scholars' Speech," August 30, 2021, www.insidehighered.com/
news/2021/08/31/fire-launches-new-database-tracking-attacks-
speech.

Public shaming and bullying can be dished out by conservatives as
well. See, for example, Ben Burgis, "Publicly Shamed," *Jacobin*, April 9,
2020, jacobin.com/2020/09/publicly-shamed-jon-ronson-cancel-cul-
ture. As many argue, they have their own brand of cancel culture, whether
related to drag shows or books. For a piece that takes this perspective, see
Steve Israel, "The Cancel Culture of the Right," *Hill*, February 16, 2022,
thehill.com/opinion/civil-rights/594423-the-cancel-culture-of-the-right.

For more on FIRE's lawsuit over the blocking of the charity drag
show, see "Lawsuit: FIRE Sues Texas University President Illegally Blocking Charity Drag Show," FIRE, March 24, 2023, www.thefire.org/news/
lawsuit-fire-sues-texas-university-president-illegally-blocking-chari-
ty-drag-show; and William Melhado, "Federal Judge Sides with West Texas A&M University President Who Canceled Campus Drag Show," *Texas
Tribune*, September 22, 2023, www.texastribune.org/2023/09/22/tex-
as-drag-show-west-texas-ruling.

For a discussion about the strength of science—and the limitations of
scientists—particularly as it pertains to the question of objectivity, see Josh-
ua Rothman, "How Does Science Really Work," *New Yorker*, September
28, 2020, www.newyorker.com/magazine/2020/10/05/how-does-
science-really-work.

# 1 Build Your Own Community

## The Lessons of Maria Tusken

*We've created our own little community now, so we're not
in this giant community, trying to appease everyone.*

—*Maria Tusken*

These days, when the digital world offers something for anyone but
nothing for everyone, there's no shortage of stories of online communities gone toxic. After all, it's far easier for one person to initiate a pile-on
against a faceless avatar than it is for them to do the same against a real
human being in real life. It only takes the click of a button. This is all
something that Maria Tusken has become acutely aware of.

A few years ago, Tusken, who was part of the knitting community
and owner of a hand-dyed yarn business called Tuskenknits, found herself targeted by a hostile online mob. Her crime? Defending a fellow
knitter by the name of Karen Templer, a white woman who was piled on
after daring to share her excitement about an upcoming trip to India in
a blog post. In the post, Templer compared the trip to "being offered a
seat on a flight to Mars," and although initially she received encouraging
words from commentators, she was soon facing the social justice warrior
(SJW) knitting mob, who accused her of using "othering" language and

pressured her to apologize. The more she tried to dig herself out of that hole, the more the story spun out of proportion and the more the mob descended on Templer in the name of "justice" and "inclusivity."

The so-called great unraveling quickly became the number one topic of conversation. Facebook pages and YouTube channels that were ostensibly devoted to knitting techniques and tips railed against Templer. Soon, the story went mainstream. Multiple articles were written calling out this extreme instance of "racism" in the knitting community. The chorus grew louder and more vicious in its attacks. Yet, behind the scenes, watching this unfold, many in the knitting community understood that the situation was completely overblown and insane.

But they said nothing. They were too afraid.

Something about Tusken, however, made her unable to continue to observe in silence, and, sure enough, unwelcome consequences soon followed. Watching a fellow knitter being condemned and called things like "racist b*tch" and "white supremacist," she was horrified and felt like she had to do something. So she released a video and a statement on her Instagram account speaking out against the intolerant culture that had grabbed hold of her knitting community.

Within hours, if not minutes, she received a bold introduction to "cancel culture"—in the form of hateful emails. At the peak of the "controversy," she was receiving hundreds per day. The worst of the attacks lasted for a few weeks. That's about as long as social justice warriors are able to concentrate on any one "cause." Yet the effects on her psyche have been far longer lasting. Even though she no longer receives hate messages, she still has trouble looking at her email, even today.

At first, Tusken tried to respond to the people condemning her, but she soon learned that there was no conversation to be had with them. "I basically would go into my email and delete everything because I just didn't want to even see or read most of this stuff." Among the people "reaching out" were those telling her that they no longer wanted to do collaborations with her—something essential for business growth within her sector. She also had real-life friends telling her that they didn't want to be seen in public with her.

Given the behavior of the mob, no one could show support without putting their own standing within the community and source of income at risk. For example, when another woman commented positively on Tusken's video, agreeing with her, the mob promptly contacted the woman's employer to politely let them know that she should be fired because she was associated with a "white supremacist"—that is, Tusken.

The woman told Tusken about this unfolding situation, confiding in her about the sheer insanity of this as well as how scared she was feeling. Tusken responded, agreeing and thanking her for her support, but did not hear back. A few days later, the woman posted a YouTube video in which she denounced Tusken. "I'm sure they were basically holding her hostage until she did this," says Tusken.

Eventually, Tusken began to get other emails of support, but people were too afraid to say anything in her favor publicly. Some even confessed that they had unfollowed her on social media to avoid getting attacked but wanted her to know that they still supported her. Tusken still has mixed feelings about that. She recalls a Zoom call with a husband-wife team of a popular knitting channel on YouTube. The wife cried on the call. "I don't know what to do," she told Tusken. "I want to publicly support you, but I don't know what to do." Their entire livelihood was at stake.

In the background, there was no shortage of people who felt bad about what happened, including other prominent people in the knitting community, but they were not willing to take the risk and speak up. Meanwhile, their businesses grew, whereas Tusken's stagnated. "But I get it," she says.

When we hear stories of people standing up for others or speaking up, knowing that there will be a price to pay, we often think that these individuals are courageous— perhaps just a little bit braver than we are. How do we find and bottle that elusive and exotic ingredient?

For Tusken, courage did not play as significant a role as her moral sense of right and wrong and her willingness to value that above one's own comforts.

"I think actually more of the courage comes after you do this," Tusken says. "It's not really courageous to actually come out against these things. It is just like this really intense feeling . . . I can't, like, look back on that time and see myself doing anything different. I can't see myself just going along with this."

There are many reasons that people are afraid of speaking up, but the dominant ones tend to be (1) not wanting to be ostracized and attacked by their "tribe" and (2) not having a safety net when it comes to losing one's job or business—especially for those who have families to support.

"It's easier if you're just an individual, but I don't know how you could live with yourself if what you're doing is going against your conscience," says Tusken. "Integrity is really, really important to me." It's something that was instilled in her by her family from an early age, along with some help from old classic novels by authors like Charles Dickens and Jane Austen. "They're all about living with integrity."

Tusken still gets emails from people telling her they are thankful that someone spoke up. What transpired split the knitting community. Given the current cultural climate, it was inevitable. "It was bound to happen at some point," says Tusken. "And I'm really glad that it split and that I was actually one of the leaders of that split. We've created our own little community now, so we're not in this giant community, trying to appease everyone."

Building smaller communities is the answer for some. Tusken says that many of the people she knows have begun to treat their social media profiles kind of like dating profiles. They will intentionally put their gender or pronouns, political beliefs, and religion in the bio—almost like a shield that lets people know who they are. It essentially says: if you don't like me, don't follow me—because I don't want to get attacked. "Everyone has sort of created these little microcosms and groups that way." Her advice? Find a community that aligns with your values so that when you decide that you want to be brave and speak up about something of importance, you've got a group of people who aren't going to shun you.

For Tusken, knitting had been her life and obsession. Thus, all of her friends were not only in the knitting community but also had their livelihoods tied to it, so when Tusken was targeted by the online mob, no one was willing to offer public support. The true believers didn't want to be associated with her, while those who thought the mob had overreacted *couldn't* be associated with her. She learned a truly painful lesson: "I kind of realized that most of those people weren't actual friends, and I've since made different friends—true friends." Looking back, she wishes she had trusted her gut more. "There was sort of an uneasiness, always, with these friends. Like I couldn't truly be myself or express my opinions." She has since become more selective with her friends, and as an introverted person, she doesn't feel like she needs many. Instead, she is thankful for the people she has in her life now.

Unlike Karen Templer, who ended up apologizing for perpetuating "the harmful notion that Indians (and POC in general) are 'other,'" Tusken chose not to apologize for her own words, even though people in her life were telling her how dire the situation was and that she needed to do something. "I was pretty silent for like a week or two," she recalls, "I just felt like there literally was nothing for me to apologize for, and it would have been going against my own conscience if I [did]." You can't make everyone online happy. "Also, all of these people going after me, I wasn't affecting them and their lives, and the things that I said had nothing to do with them. They were the ones making this big deal out of it." Even so, staying quiet was difficult because she wanted to defend herself and prove that she was not any of the words they called her, but she knew that would be a mistake. The stove was on, and she didn't want to raise the temperature any further.

But although Tusken retained her exterior strength, nothing about her newly found circumstances felt stable. "It was such a new thing to me, and I had no idea what was going on in the world politically, so it was just really shocking." She threw up one morning just from the anxiety of it all. "I just woke up one morning, read an email from a friend, and then went and threw up."

After being interviewed by a YouTube channel called "Unsafe Space," she was inspired by the hosts' brave willingness to talk about anything, including the well-documented hypocrisy of so many who call themselves social justice warriors. They might talk endlessly about "inclusivity" and "tolerance," but she wanted to expose them for what they truly are: bullies. Noticing the same language and lingo choice that kept popping up in the bullying attacks on her, Tusken decided to create a line of yarns inspired by their words—words like "privilege" and "microaggression" and "emotional labor." She dubbed the collection "Polarized Knits." "Even a year after this had happened, everyone was still being really careful and keeping their heads down, so I thought this could be a really good business opportunity for me to actually be the first one to make fun of them and make money."

Of course, this got the social justice warriors very angry, which didn't keep Tusken from selling a lot of yarn to new fans. Things were different this time because not only was Tusken better prepared for the backlash, but she had also built up a supportive community around her. She received plenty of negative comments on her social channels, but this time, all her supporters did all of the arguing with them—she stayed out of it and witnessed. "It was actually kind of entertaining to watch. And it was empowering."

The followers she managed to retain and attract despite everything were loyal, even if her community was now much smaller than the one she was so easily and quickly cast out of. This allowed her to make a living even after her exile, and that's something that Tusken has been grateful for. "It kind of shows that you don't need everyone to like you if you run your own business. You don't need hundreds of thousands of people to like you—you only need maybe a thousand diehard fans." Yet, although that base of support provided enough for her immediate needs, Tusken's overall business continued to suffer and be stagnant in other ways, as the mob continued to cast a long shadow. An outcast from the broader community, she found that she was unable to grow her knitting business through all-important collaborations, for example.

In some ways, the online bully mob is a symptom of the Internet age we live in. We went from being connected to a limited number of individuals we've curated into our lives, to millions of strangers who suddenly get a say. "The Internet is still so new, and we're still really learning how to deal with it," says Tusken. "It's kind of given me just a little bit of perspective on being a bit gentler with myself and other people because we're all learning how to use this new technology. I think in twenty or thirty years, we'll be using the Internet a lot differently."

Tusken can't imagine this happening in real life in the same way. "I'm one of those people in real life [that] when people pick on me, I just completely ignore them." Being homeschooled until sixth grade gave her a strong sense of self ("I was pretty immune to what people thought of me"), and having three older brothers who constantly picked on her as a child taught her that if she paid no attention to the taunts, those doing the taunting would stop. Besides, it's much harder to be mean directly to someone's face than behind a keyboard.

Although Tusken found a new community and managed to hold on to her small yarn business for a while, she no doubt paid a hefty price. Given the costs, it's hard not to ask, why shouldn't someone like her remain silent?

"What price does society pay when people are silent?" she answers. The Overton Window has shifted so much and so quickly over the past few years because regular everyday people have remained silent—they've abdicated their duty, hopeful that others will take all the risk and punishment while they maintain their safety. "It has totally shifted to where the craziest in our society, which are the loudest, are the ones controlling everything." That's the price: a world gone mad.

In the meantime, we must strive to build the communities we want to see in the world—no matter how small. As the infamous line from the film *Field of Dreams* goes, "If you build it, they will come." Building new, better communities, as well as institutions, is the antidote to the toxic ones. It provides a home for those who feel homeless. It gives strength of numbers—albeit initially modest—to those who feel alone. These expanding self-made alternative communities can have tremendous power when it comes to laying a foundation for the future we want to manifest and fostering an environment that nurtures free expression, individuality, freedom, and respectful discourse.

Unfortunately, not all stories have happy endings. In November 2022, Tusken sent out an email to her customers telling them that she was selling out her stock and closing her store. She gave no explanation for this decision, and she did not return a follow-up email from this author. Her storefront's website has since been shuttered, and her social media account is set to private. On Reddit, this news was gleefully celebrated by Tusken's detractors.

## Notes

Tusken's story was covered by a number of media outlets and unleashed a firestorm of comments on Reddit and elsewhere, but as one journalist wrote: "Don't we all have better things to be doing with our time?" See Poppy Noor, "Knitting Influencer Gets in a Tangle after Mocking Wokeness with Yarn," *Guardian*, February 20, 2020, www.theguardian.com/lifeand-style/2020/feb/20/knitting-influencer-wokeness-maria-tusken).

In the aftermath of Tusken's cancellation, she was featured as one of three people whose lives were transformed by "cancel culture" in a story by Taylor Mooney and Justin Sherman: "How 'Cancel Culture' Changed These Three Lives Forever," CBS News, April 12, 2022, www.cbsnews.com/news/cancel-culture-changed-lives-forever-cbsn-originals.

BuzzFeed's Tanya Chen covered the "SJW Yarns" that Tusken released to mock the cultural phenomenon: "A Micro Influencer in The Knitting Instagram Community Incited A Lot Of Drama After Naming Her Yarn 'SJW' Terms," *BuzzFeed News*, February 19, 2020, www.buzzfeednews.com/article/tanyachen/knitting-micro-influencer-drama-naming-yarn-sjw-terms.

Tusken has spoken publicly about her experience in long-form interviews on a few occasions. She shared her story and perspective on Unsafe Space's YouTube show *Deprogrammed*: "Surviving an SJW Invasion w/ Maria Tusken," YouTube, live streamed on October 3, 2019, www.youtube.com/watch?v=up7JgDsvrhI. She also spoke with Politically Incorrect Knitters about what life is like post-cancellation: "Episode 11: Special Guest Maria Tusken." YouTube, video uploaded by Politically Incorrect Knitters on August 15, 2020, www.youtube.com/watch?v=m57fDoiCNuE.

# 2 Don't Seek Approval from Bullies

## The Lessons of Kat Rosenfield

*It seems as though people don't genuinely believe in this stuff,
but they don't want to experience the blowback that comes
from expressing the majority opinion. And so this very small
but very loud, and sorry—but very, very crazy minority—
is able to kind of dominate the conversation.*

*—Kat Rosenfield*

When the Young Adult fiction mob came after author and journalist Kat
Rosenfield, as unsettling as it was to be dogpiled online, the experience
also brought out her natural journalistic curiosity. What's going on here,
she wondered.

It was around 2014 when the young adult fiction world started to
become quite obsessed with ideas around diversity. A few years later,
what started as a genuine push for diversity in an industry that needed
it was now being mobilized to push out writers that certain individuals
weren't particularly fond of. This was done under the guise that they were
"taking up space that could have gone to somebody more 'deserving,'"
says Rosenfield. That this more 'deserving' candidate tended to be either
the individual doing the pushing out or one of their friends didn't go un-

noticed. "It was very high school," says Rosenfield. "There was a clique of four women, and if you traced it back, anytime there was one of these big blow-ups, it would always be one of them." Together, they functioned as a very efficient machine for organizing take-downs of people that they "perceived as needing that to happen to them."

Around that time, a Facebook group for women writers called Binders emerged, and it grew to be rather large and influential, with over 40,000 members. Subgroups were formed, and one of those was dedicated to Young Adult writers, of which Rosenfield was a member. She spotted a petition that was being circulated in the group to try to get a forthcoming book, *The Continent* by Keira Drake, pulled because the one person in the group who had read it declared that it was racist. It was very strategic, recalls Rosenfield. "The discussion was: Let's get this petition going, let's all sign it and say we just want it pulled for edits, but then, because we know how publishing works, it will allow them to just quietly cancel it later. Basically, writers were conspiring to censor somebody else's work."

There's an interesting phenomenon in play whereby a group of people can gain quite a bit of power, as well as social and cultural capital, by claiming not to have any, Rosenfield explains. As she was witnessing in real time, it can be a rather effective strategy. People were saying that others had to listen to them and do what they demanded because they were "powerless." It's a cynical move, but in many cases, they truly believe themselves to be powerless—to be victims. If they see themselves as the ones who are oppressed, if they see themselves as the righteous ones, "they become quite empowered to do harm to other people's career." They never consider they are—or even could be—the oppressor.

Rosenfield took to Twitter. Without naming anybody or even the book itself, she posted about how it's really rather strange to see a group of creative professionals advocating for book banning in the name of social justice.

This was sufficient to disturb the hornet's nest. "There was like this machine that kicked into gear. It was very aggressive and it was very organized," she recalls. Rosenfield had to be shut down. Never mind that she was not even remotely a prominent figure at the time and had at most 1,500 followers on Twitter. She was still deemed a threat and had to be destroyed.

But Rosenfield's original tweet wasn't enough to bring her down, so someone went on to accuse her of having a sock puppet account that she used to send racist abuse to women of color on Twitter. "It was just completely false." The account she was accused of running had shared a screenshot from the Young Adult Facebook group, something against the group's rules, and so Rosenfield was kicked out of the group—despite having zero connection to the account.

"Obviously, this is a really damaging rumor to have somebody spread about you, especially in a space like Young Adult fiction, where everyone is very, very avid about ostracizing people who seem to have run afoul of the norms in some way," she says. "So, once that rumor was out there, it was like red meat for that crowd." It didn't matter that it was verifiably false—for starters, if you examine the timestamps, you'd realize that Rosenfield couldn't have been the person tweeting since she was in the woods with no cell service at the time. "But it just took off because it was a narrative. It was like, 'Hey, here's an opportunity for you to destroy the life of somebody you already don't like. So that was how it kind of caught fire."

Once stories begin to spread on the Internet, it's nearly impossible to stop or correct them. When Rosenfield asked those with larger followings who were spreading the story to stop sharing lies, the "community" declared that she was behaving abusively and attacking "these brave women who outed her as the monster she is."

Rosenfield believes that these sorts of pile-ons tend to attract a certain personality type—a personality disorder, even. Narcissists are particularly drawn toward using a form of gaslighting called DARVO, which stands for deny, attack, and reverse victim and offender. In essence, the actual perpetrator will accuse the person they've victimized of doing the bad thing to them—thereby turning themselves into the victim. "It was basically like that. Something bad has happened to you, and you speak out about it, and you become the offender by speaking out about it."

In a grotesque inversion of reality, they continue to be "powerless," and anything they might do to you is fully justified because you are the "powerful."

Just like that, Rosenfield became radioactive. The editor who had published Rosenfield's first two books unfollowed her on Twitter, as did many other colleagues in the Young Adult space, and she received a storm of abusive tweets directed at her. "Nobody would defend me."

The silence hurt, particularly when it came from people she knew in real life. "I remember reaching out to one woman who I was really friends with. I sent her a message and I was like: 'We've had drinks together, we've hung out in real life a number of times, are you going to say anything about this?'" She responded: "I don't know what you're talking about." She never spoke to Rosenfield again.

"There was a moment of real despair when this rumor first started circulating," Rosenfield recalls. "I was like, I think this is it, I think that I'm not going to be able to do the thing that I'm good at anymore, ever again . . . Obviously, that was personally unsettling," she says, but she also couldn't help but wonder what is going on in this community that's allowing this dynamic to take hold.

Others were noticing, too. "I did start getting a lot of messages from people who were like, 'This is completely out of control, and I'm terrified to say anything publicly. I'm too scared that I'll be next.'"

Once Rosenfield started looking into this trend more, she was surprised to discover that this went further than just a bunch of authors trying to censor and bully fellow authors. "I found a bunch of middle-aged professional women censoring and bullying teenagers who were their readership who were not toeing the line properly when it came to, you know, promoting books that had progressive political values. If a teenage girl on the Internet said, 'I'd like to read this book that's being taken out so I can form my own opinion about it,' a forty-year-old woman with publishing contracts, like the authors that the girl read and admired, would go after her and tell her she was a racist and tell her this was disgusting."

Once Rosenfield had realized just how many branches there were on that tree, she was fascinated by that dynamic and decided that she had to write about this. Her article "The Toxic Drama on YA Twitter," published by *Vulture* in August 2017, ended up being the most viral piece she had ever written. It talked about how Young Adult books were being dragged on social media, sometimes before anybody's even read them, and how teenage girls were being targeted by the authors they admire just for professing the mildest interest in the "wrong" books.

"Obviously, people came after me when I published this reported piece because it pulled up the lid on a lot of toxic stuff that was happening in the community. The people whose bad behavior was being reported on for a broader audience suddenly found themselves being scrutinized by people who were not in their clique and not sympathetic to them."

The day the piece came out, Rosenfield's husband texted her with updates. She was afraid to even look at what was happening. Turns out, everyone was sharing the article. "It was very gratifying and very vindicating." Readers agreed that this phenomenon was clearly both as insane and as fascinating as Rosenfield had suspected.

Back then, a piece like this could still squeeze by. Today, perhaps this is not as likely, as ideological capture is increased within legacy media, notes Rosenfield.

"It seems as though people don't genuinely believe in this stuff, but they don't want to experience the blowback that comes from expressing the majority opinion. And so this very small but very loud, and sorry—but very, very crazy minority—is able to kind of dominate the conversation."

When Rosenfield began to write about this subject, there appeared to be a very organized campaign to block her and dissuade people from talking to her. "When somebody did talk to me, she was like, I have to be anonymous, or I'll be blackballed. Obviously, there was a lot of social pressure there."

As for Rosenfield, she admits that she's never really been very good at keeping her mouth shut, nor has she really been able to participate when it's been socially convenient to espouse views she doesn't believe in. "This has been a consistent theme throughout my life."

Still, she doesn't feel like she holds any particularly controversial opinions and sees herself primarily as an onlooker: "I feel like I spend a lot of time kind of observing things, kicking over rocks and pointing at what's under there . . . Even now, I don't really do a lot of judging [in my writing]. I just do a lot of pointing: this is a thing that is happening."

In the wake of that drama, Rosenfield says that she has a pretty robust offline life, and as she has begun to do more cultural and social commentary, she has found a group of people who aren't interested in the hysteria, people with whom she can have more honest relationships with, even online. "I've never really been a person who has a group. I have a handful of relationships with people who are very dear to me, who, were they to criticize me, I would take that seriously."

When accusations come flying in with such conviction—at least the not made-up ones—it can be hard not to consider that they might have some sort of point. "Yeah, I definitely had a moment where . . . I mean, obviously, if somebody calls you racist, the first thing you think is like, 'Oh, God, am I?' And the thing was that, you know, after a few days of this and seeing how these people behaved, I was like, do I care if this person who is tweeting like the most vitriolic, horrible shit at a stranger over and over . . . do I care if this person thinks badly of me? No, [even] this person's good opinion would not be a compliment. I don't want that person to think well of me."

That was a liberating realization. "People who are behaving in this way aren't the people whose approval I want. There's something off about them . . . I just got really comfortable with the idea that this group of somewhat unhinged people thinks that I'm a racist."

For Rosenfield, that's fine. She knows that she's not and does not require their approval. She describes being tribeless as a bit of a super-power. "I have never cultivated friendships with a group of people who would reject me for expressing a viewpoint that goes against the grain or for asking for nuance." Those who belong to an ideological or moral "tribe," on the other hand, might enjoy a surface-level safety in numbers, but in truth, they are extremely vulnerable. They are subject to the same forces that drove Rosenfield out of the Young Adult writing community. This real and present fear of being rejected or dragged into the mud can make them more fearful of speaking up.

As for the sock-puppet account attributed to Rosenfield, Rosenfield says that the real owner has since been in touch, and the person felt really bad about the situation—just not bad enough to admit it was them. "But I don't really blame her for that." She continues, "I had this fascinating exchange where I was like, 'You are scapegoating me. Can we just admit that you're scapegoating me?' And she just refused to do it."

When Rosenfield was ousted from the Young Adult Facebook group, her close friend Leigh Stein, who at the time was one of the moderators of the main group and helping to run a nonprofit conference that existed under its umbrella, told the Young Adult group's moderator that she was making a mistake and that the accusations were absolute nonsense. The Young Adult moderator responded: "It must be so painful to know that your friend would do something like this." This was a defining moment for Stein: if she couldn't stand up for a close friend, who was she? She quit the group. After she left, Stein went on to write *Self Care: A Novel*, which is set in the wellness industry and happens to be a satire about women who destroy other women in the name of "feminism."

"I certainly got Leigh in the divorce from Binders," quips Rosenfield. "I definitely got the better end of the deal there."

Yet, this hasn't stopped the bullies—or bullying. The people with the same types of personality disorders—if not the very same people—continue to deliver the pain in the name of some warped form of justice. "I see that happening in media-dominant spaces. Media Twitter is an absolute snake pit of people just sniping and being catty to each other and turning on each other." The moment someone writes a piece that runs afoul of the orthodoxy within their tribe, everyone turns on them, earning clout by joining in on the pile-on. It's a quick way to learn who your friends are.

That's why, again, argues Rosenfield, cultivating a small circle of loyal friends whose opinions you care about and trust is key. They can be honest in their criticism but never cruel. These are the people you listen to, and you just ignore everyone else.

"I think, in general, people need to just get less afraid of being dragged on Twitter. It's totally survivable. You'll be okay." At the end of the day, someone has to go first and break the seal. "If you're the first one to say something, everybody else will start saying stuff too. Right now, the fear is palpable, and it's certainly limiting how much conversation can take place."

Today, Rosenfield no longer writes within the Young Adult space, but she is now writing adult fiction and continues to be a prolific and opinionated writer on all sorts of topics. She also knows that many of her peers haven't survived the "snake pit" nearly as well. Some were unable to stand up to their bullies—unapologetically—and therefore were trampled over. Others have a crippling fear preventing them from ever unlocking their authentic voices. But expression doesn't belong in a cage, and a few radical voices should not dictate what the rest of society is or isn't allowed to talk about. However, until more people stop paying attention to those bulling voices, until they stop seeking their approval, the bullies will continue to have power.

That power disappears when they are ignored by enough of the silenced majority. It isn't real unless we make it so.

**Notes**

Rosenfield hasn't been afraid to tackle some pretty sensitive topics, no matter the format or platform, whether in her writing, in public discussions, or on social media. For her infamous article about the toxicity within the Young Adult world, see: "The Toxic Drama of YA on Twitter," *New York Magazine*, Vulture, August 2017, www.vulture.com/2017/08/the-toxic-drama-of-ya-twitter.html. Her own experiences have also led her to write more broadly about cancel culture and how its central problem is that it causes us to lose trust in each other: "The Real Problem with Cancel Culture," *Tablet*, October 15, 2019, www.tabletmag.com/sections/news/articles/real-problem-with-cancel-culture.

In an interview by Nick Gillespie, she is equally fearless: "Stan Lee Co-author Kat Rosenfield on Rise of Cancel Culture in the Literary World," *Reason*, September 11, 2019, reason.com/podcast/2019/09/11/stan-lee-co-author-kat-rosenfield-on-rise-of-cancel-culture-in-the-literary-world.

She's well worth following on X (formerly known as Twitter), where she is quite active under the handle @katrosenfield. She also hosts a podcast called Feminine Chaos (femchaospod.substack.com).

# 3 Talk to Everyone, Even "Awful People"

## The Lessons of Daryl Davis

*I want people to come together and say whatever they want to say—even if it's not something that I agree with or something that I can support—and be able to feel safe, not like someone's going to attack them, or they have to walk on eggshells.*

—*Daryl Davis*

Is anyone beyond a conversation? These days, people are so quick to dismiss others as being unworthy of conversation. Maybe they are stupid. Somewhat racist. Or worst of all, Republican. These days, many people don't want to have Christmas and Thanksgiving together because of who their family—siblings even—voted for.

Meanwhile, there's an African American man named Daryl Davis who has spent considerable time engaging with members of the Ku Klux Klan (KKK) and neo-Nazis. "If you can't talk to your own family, something is wrong here," he says.

Born in 1958, Davis isn't a stranger to a time when massive discrimination based on the color of his skin wasn't merely commonplace; it was also legal. A musician, activist, author, and actor, Davis has become particularly well-known for collecting robes and hoods—gifted to him by men who left and denounced the KKK thanks to him.

Davis's unique journey began with a chance encounter in 1983 when he was playing country western music at a bar in Maryland. A white man came up to him and gave him a peculiar compliment: he'd never heard a black man play as well as Jerry Lee Lewis. Davis—who had played with not only Jerry Lee Lewis but also Chuck Berry and B. B. King—patiently explained that "Jerry Lee learned to play from black blues and boogie-woogie piano players" and was a friend of his. After a few drinks, the man revealed to Davis that he was a member of the KKK. Yet, their discussion didn't end then and there. Surprisingly, the two eventually became unlikely friends.

At the core of what drives Davis is a question he's had all the way from his youth: "Why do you hate me when you know nothing about me?" He's been asking that question for nearly four decades. Davis's curiosity about what might lead someone to hold racist beliefs is integral to his willingness to have open conversations.

Davis credits his broader perspective to his upbringing. Born in Chicago, Davis's father was a foreign service officer, so he grew up as a U.S. Embassy kid. Beginning at the age of three, he'd end up in a new country every few years. His classmates at the international schools he attended were from all over the world—kids from Nigeria, Japan, Turkey, Germany, Denmark—you name it.

"So that became my baseline, all these different ethnicities and colors and cultures and ideologies, I thought that was the norm," recalls Davis. "But every time I'd come home, at the end of my dad's assignment, I would either be in the still-segregated all-black schools or the newly integrated black and white schools."

Davis recalls the black-and-white televisions of the past and the awe many felt when color television came into play. "Well, for me, it was the reverse," he says. "Coming home from overseas was like going from color TV to black and white because there was, like, no diversity in this country." Whereas most people around him lived in their little bubbles and didn't really travel outside them, Davis grew up being around different people, ideologies, languages, and customs. He grew up with it.

"I think because I traveled so much and was exposed to so many different things, [the way I view] Trump supporters or Biden supporters or whatever supporters, that's just another culture."

So, what reasons might a Klansman give for hating Davis and other minorities?

"He'll say, well, Mr. Davis, you know, black people are prone to crime." He'd claim that this is supported by evidence—for example, that there are more black people in prison than there are white people. "He sees that data—he sees those statistics—and of course, it fits his already bigoted mind. So he doesn't look any further."

In other words, he would have reached his conclusion first and then sought evidence to justify his conclusion second.

But if he did investigate further, what would he find?

"Well, there is an imbalance in our judicial system in this country that sends black people to prison when it sends white people home, or it imposes longer sentences for black people than it does for white people who have committed the same crime."

Ignoring these other explanations for the data, he might further explain that not only are black people more prone to crime, but that they are also inherently lazy. "We don't want to work. We prefer to scam the government welfare system. We always have our handout for some free program or freebie or whatever. And then he tells me that black people are born with a smaller brain than white people. And the larger the brain, the more capacity for intelligence; the smaller the brain, the lower the IQ."

His evidence? The fact that year after year, consistently, black kids score lower on the SATs (Scholastic Assessment Tests). "And he's right," admits Davis. "Black kids overall in this country scored lower than white kids on those aptitude tests."

The data supports his racist ideology, and he doesn't look any further.

He's got the statistics to back him up.

But, what he doesn't realize is that most black kids in the United States go to school in the inner city, whereas most white kids go to schools in the suburbs—which are better funded and have more resources. "I can guarantee you that black kids who go to school in the suburbs score just as high if not higher than some of the white kids who go to school in the inner city. It has absolutely nothing to do with their skin color."

But, when someone is looking at this through a certain lens, they are just seeking to reinforce their belief—they only look for whatever it is that supports their mission.

And why wouldn't they? Doubt is something people often have difficulty with. Having certainty is more comfortable, particularly if their tribe supports the narrative of that certainty. Doubt puts them in an uncomfortable position.

Still, how does one get to a point where they become so rooted in certain beliefs that they willingly join the KKK? Understanding them is important to Davis because, as he says, they are not all "cut from a standard cookie cutter."

They come from different walks of life, socioeconomic statuses, and educational backgrounds. People in the Klan have ranged from third-grade dropouts all the way to powerful politicians.

What Davis learned is that there was no one reason that someone might join. In some cases, it was a family tradition that had been passed down from one generation to the next. Or, if you found yourself as a new resident of a small rural town with a strong Klan presence, there might have been pressure to join. "Particularly as an outsider coming into a place where everybody knows everyone and is suspicious of outsiders. So you assimilate, to be accepted."

There are also many stories of depressed towns, like coal-mining towns. "Working in mining is good money–but one day the company gets greedy and starts hiring immigrants to save money, laying off workers. They see them as a literal threat to their livelihood. They often don't start out racist, but they are in trouble and they can't afford to feed their family. And the Klan will see it and come into town, hold a rally, and they'll tell them: the black people have NAACP and Jews have the ADL, but nobody stands up for the white man. But the KKK will help you get your job back."

There are many people, says Davis, who were never racists to begin with but who found themselves in a situation where they couldn't feed their family, put clothes on their kids' backs, or pay their mortgage. They think: "What do they have to lose? Give me an application and sign me up." They are in such despair they are willing to go along with anything.

For members of the KKK and other white supremacist and neo-Nazi groups, there's also a fear of their identity being erased. "What these people tell me is, Daryl, I don't want my grandkids to be brown—they call it the browning of America or white genocide." And there's some truth to it; the white population is indeed dropping.

Even understanding some of the reasoning behind why people might join such groups, it isn't easy to get around viewing them with the openness that Davis has. After all, many of the views they hold are truly despicable. And yet, understanding their motives and circumstances can be key to change.

There are a number of stories of people who were Klansman or neo-Nazis and now dedicate their lives to undoing the damage they've done and getting others out. It reminds us that, even among seemingly the worst of humans, there's a chance for redemption. Given the right circumstances—be it depression, loneliness, or poverty some people are capable of falling into any community that will have them. A community that will reassure them that this is not their fault and that they are not alone. They are not necessarily bad humans, but they are desperate and susceptible. And yet, perhaps they are still capable of seeing their way out.

But one way that can't happen, Davis notes, is through attack or ridicule. That is not how people change their minds. It's how they dive further into the fringes and extremes. So, how *do* you change minds?

"One's perception is their reality," explains Davis. "Even if it's not real, it's still their reality." And you cannot change somebody's reality.

"If you attack someone's reality, you will hit a brick wall because they are going to defend it. All they know is what they know. And if it's real to them, that's enough." The more you attack their reality, the more resistance you're going to find—which can boil into anger and even violence. "So what you want to do is, rather than attack their reality, offer them a better perception. Because one's perception is one's reality. So if you give them a better perception, and they resonate with your perception, they will change their own reality."

Davis presents the following scenario: Let's say you have a younger brother who comes home from a magic show and keeps going on about how he saw a woman get cut in half with a chainsaw. You try to explain that it's an illusion, but your brother insists that he saw it with his own eyes. That's his reality, and when you tell him it isn't real—you're attacking his reality. So, naturally, he's going to defend it. You're wasting your time trying to change his reality.

Instead, insists Davis, offering him a better perception is the key.

"You say to him: 'Hey, I hear what you're saying. I understand what you're saying. But is it possible that perhaps, when the magician on stage asked for a female volunteer, he picked out one that worked for him, and you don't realize it because she's just part of the audience? So when she comes up on stage, and he has her get in the box, there is already a pair of mannequin legs lying on the floor of the box that are wearing the same stockings and same shoes as she has on? So she takes those legs and sticks them out the hole and brings her own knees up under her chest, so when he cuts the box in half, the saw never even touches her? So then, when he separates the two boxes over there, it's just a pair of dummy legs?"

What you've now offered him is a better perception that can resonate with him and allow him to change his own reality. "We should always come up with better perceptions, and then people will change their own reality. Because as soon as you try to compel somebody to do something, there's going to be pushback."

Although Davis has taken an active role in engaging with those who might hold truly abhorrent views, there are many who wouldn't wish to do the same, and Davis doesn't believe that he has an obligation to as a private citizen. But, he says, "I am of the mindset that our country can only become one of two things: it can become one that which we just sit back and watch it become, or it can become to that which we stand up and make it become. So, as citizens of this country, we all have to ask ourselves, do I want to sit back and see what my country becomes? Or do I want to stand up and make my country become what I want to see? I've chosen the latter. I'm not obligated to do that. But that's what I feel I need to do now."

However, unlike himself, Davis believes that elected officials like senators and congressmen *do* have an obligation to sit down and talk with people with whom they disagree. Why? Because they do not represent just one particular group; they represent everybody in their district—and they can disagree with one another. They can have different opinions. "So as a representative, you have an obligation to represent all the people and try to bring unity together. It's okay to disagree. It's okay to feel differently and do different things. But we must agree to get along. And as an elected official, it's your obligation to bring people together to maintain the peace and tranquility of your city, of your state, of your country, of your town. That's how I feel."

There's been an increasing sense of tribalism in recent years. Many people are afraid of speaking openly, even within their own in-groups. "You're either with us or you're against us, and you can't be halfway. You either agree with the whole thing, or you are the enemy. You either accept all of our doctrine, not just pages one, three, and five, but all ten pages, or you need to go. People are afraid of expressing their opinion—[particularly] if it's slightly to the right or center of the left—they are afraid they will get ostracized. So they just want to, you know, walk the straight and narrow, and they're either quiet or they're completely outspoken in that particular direction."

What's the solution? "Tell people to grow a pair of balls," exclaims Davis. "Get them to realize [that they've] got a voice." This is especially true in a country like the United States, Davis says, which "was built on freedom of speech" and where "you have a right to your beliefs."

And yet, there's another mechanism of censorship at play. When the Dixie Chicks criticized George W. Bush in 2003 for the Allied invasion of Iraq, for example, radio stations suddenly stopped playing their records and they lost gigs. People weren't merely disagreeing with them—they felt that they should pay a price for having a particular opinion. "That's not right," says Davis.

Throughout the years, we've seen this trend implode into what many call "cancel culture." Most opponents of cancel culture don't see it as simply being "accountability culture," whereby bad behaviors have just consequences. Instead, they see it as a growing intolerance toward those who express views or ask questions outside the orthodoxy. Since both traditional and social media tend to favor spectacle, these extreme voices get further amplified and carry disproportionate power to silence and intimidate, which makes them impossible to ignore. So bad ideas, bad players, and bad behaviors get elevated presence on the social stage. Those who disagree are often too scared to speak out, giving the impression that they, too, hold such beliefs.

But what to do with those views that are truly bigoted or even dangerous, like the beliefs held by the people Davis regularly engages with? In other words, shouldn't those who traffic in blatantly racist speech be silenced? "You can't address something until you see it," says Davis. Or hear it.

"So you know, if you're driving down the street in your car, and your car starts making some kind of weird noise under the hood . . . you're not a mechanic, what do you do? You drive to the auto repair place and say: 'Hey, can you look at my car? It's making some weird noise.' So the mechanic comes out and says, 'Start your car.' You start the car, and the noise isn't there, of course. So he says, 'Well, let me drive it around the block.' He gets in the driver's seat and drives around, no noise. He tells you: 'Well, listen, I can't fix what I can't hear.' So with racism in this country, it's hard to fix when it's hidden under the carpet behind the door, locked in the closet."

Having conversations with people who hold racist views doesn't mean you are endorsing their point of view. For Davis, it is a way of holding them to account through dialogue. "I want people to come together and say whatever they want to say—even if it's not something that I agree with or something that I can support—and be able to feel safe, not like someone's going to attack them, or they have to walk on eggshells." Regardless of whether they share the same opinion on things like abortion, climate change, or cancel culture, he aims to create an actual safe space—not the kind where one can talk only about things that won't offend anyone else.

What does such a space look like in practice? Allow people to make their point without interruption and give them an equal amount of minutes, says Davis. "You can express your [honest] views if that's what you believe, but you cannot directly attack someone because of their religion or the color of their skin. Or whether they believe in God or they're atheist . . . that's not going to be a productive conversation." State your facts or logical argument, regardless of whether others agree, but do not directly attack.

These days, of course, people are quick to attack. Calling someone a racist, bigot, or Nazi is a favorite pastime for some. But even if someone is truly worthy of such an epithet, it may not be the best approach.

"I'd rather be antiracism than be antiracist," explains Davis. "I'd rather be pro-human. The racist, that is a learned behavior. That person was not born racist. He or she develops from their environment, whether it was their family, their workplace, or whatever [their] circumstance. We all are human beings, so let's try to address [what we need to correct] in a pro-human way."

Turns out, even Davis was once called a white supremacist by an "antiracist" group. "There you go," he smiles ironically.

Davis, who is on the board of advisors of a group called Minds, a decentralized social network, was invited to speak at a large conference the group had organized in New Jersey. It had rented a theater for the conference, the aim of which was to figure out how we as a society can deradicalize. Specifically, how can we come together and still maintain our beliefs without clashing violently? People from both the left and the right were going to come together to simply have conversations.

According to Davis, Antifa declared the group white supremacists and led a protest against the conference. Then, someone called the theater, threatening to bomb it. The theater canceled its contract with Minds out of fear, and the entire conference had to be moved elsewhere at the last minute to a casino about fifteen miles away. The new location was kept secret to avoid violent altercations. It worked. The conference was a success. That night, attendees gathered at a brewery down the street from the original location for an afterparty. "There were Trump supporters there, there were regular people, all kinds of people there. Everybody got along. Whether we agreed or not, we all got along."

Antifa was still across the street protesting. A reporter covering the event asked Davis what he thought about the people across the street. He responded: "You know what, I think we should invite them over to join the party. They can meet some of these people and understand that, yes, they have some different beliefs, but they're not evil people. We can all sit down and talk."

The invitation didn't go over well. "There's a bunch of white supremacists in there. We don't want to deal with them. They shouldn't even be there. They should not be given a room to have their party in," said an Antifa protester.

TALK TO EVERYONE, EVEN "AWFUL PEOPLE" • 67

The reporter responded: "Well, Daryl Davis is over there."

The response? "Daryl Davis is a white supremacist."

"When you say that, you've already lost the battle," says Davis. "I'm sorry, if that's your ammunition, you've lost."

Some people will hold on to their racist beliefs until they go to the grave, but occasionally, even the most seemingly hopeless cases can be capable of change—if given the opportunity.

"People who are willing to sit down and have a conversation, there is an opportunity to plant that seed, right?" he says. "Then you must come back and water the seed, nurture it, and maybe it will bloom, maybe it won't. There will definitely be some people who will go to their grave being hateful, violent, racist, and antisemitic; they just never change. But I've even had some people who are like that, who I thought were never going to change, later come back changed." All we can do is start the conversation.

Today, many people are unwilling to have conversations with those who might belong to another political party, let alone be members of the KKK. And yet, Davis's approach and philosophy teach us how, occasionally, even human beings who we might find truly reprehensible are often capable of change. If Davis, a Black man born in the pre–Civil Rights era, is willing to have a conversation with a Klansman, what excuse do the rest of us have when it comes to not having discourse with those with whom we simply disagree on some politics or stances like, say, abortion? Isn't it at least worth some curiosity to find out what has gotten them to believe what they do? Isn't it worth risking a conversation?

Davis is a reminder that there is hope for even the most seemingly lost among us, sometimes. And that we can have a conversation with just about anyone and live to tell the tale. Even with "awful" people.

## Notes

A great way to get some additional insight into Davis's story and perspective on why he does what he does is his TEDxNaperville talk, which has amassed over 12.5 million views as of this writing: www.ted.com/talks/ daryl_davis_why_i_as_a_black_man_attend_kkk_rallies?language=en.

He also spoke about this topic with Dwayne Brown on National Public Radio: "How One Man Convinced 200 Ku Klux Klan Members To Give Up Their Robes," NPR, *All Things Considered*, August 20, 2017, www.npr. org/2017/08/20/544861933/how-one-man-convinced-200-ku-klux- klan-members-to-give-up-their-robes.

For his explanation of why he believes that speech can combat hate, see: "Daryl Davis Combats Hate through Speech," YouTube, video uploaded by the Foundation for Individual Rights and Expression (FIRE) on July 10, 2023, www.youtube.com/watch?v=fq-l73DIUu4.

There's, of course, no shortage of articles about his work and how he's gotten more than two hundred white supremacists to change their mind. See, for example, Janice Gassam, "How Daryl Davis Inspired More Than 200 White Supremacists to Change and How His New Platform Will Help Spark Meaningful Dialogue," *Forbes*, February 29, 2020, www.forbes. com/sites/janicegassam/2020/02/29/how-daryl-davis-inspired- more-than-200-white-supremacists-to-change-and-how-his-new-plat- form-will-help-spark-meaningful-dialogue/; and Morena Duwe, "Daryl Davis: The Black Musician Who Converts Ku Klux Klan Members," *Guardian*, March 18, 2020, www.theguardian.com/music/2020/mar/18/ daryl-davis-black-musician-who-converts-ku-klux-klan-members.

You can learn more about his work in activism and beyond at his website: www.daryldavis.com.

# 4 Stick to Your Principles

## The Lessons of Stephen Elliott

*Principles matter, and you have to hold to them no matter what—*
*because if you don't—then everything starts to erode. And soon,*
*you're in a place with no morality whatsoever.*

*—Stephen Elliott*

The "Me Too" movement may have been started on social media in 2006, by activist and sexual assault survivor Tarana Burke, but it truly gained momentum once Hollywood got behind it. After allegations about producer Harvey Weinstein began to spread widely in the media, actress Alyssa Milano took to Twitter to post: "If all the women who have been sexually harassed or assaulted wrote 'Me too' as a status, we might give people a sense of the magnitude of the problem."

Turned out, the magnitude of the problem was beyond enormous, and the Me Too movement dragged it out from the shadows into the spotlight. It was a watershed moment, a collective acknowledgment of a trauma that had haunted so many. A chance to shed the shame, guilt, and secrecy. But although women (and some men) from all walks of life and careers had long suffered in helpless silence—including hotel maids and servers—particular attention was being paid to Hollywood. After all, with its glamour and notoriety, it offered the most attention-grabbing headlines. Seemingly every day, a celebrity tweeted #MeToo.

But people were sharing more than just a hashtag. Some were naming names. Famous names, even. Which only elevated the interest. Of those named, some were deserving subjects—guilty of true atrocities hidden away for years. Awful things. Things like rape or sexual assault. By now, we've all heard the many stories. As human beings, we can't help but be moved by them. The shame was no longer the victim's to carry alone.

However, as the movement intensified, some of the accusations became a bit more ambiguous to judge. Not all involved assault or abuse. Charges were made based on inappropriate comments and even a possible misunderstanding here or there. Distant sexual encounters were reconsidered and rejudged based on changing attitudes about what constitutes consent, particularly as it relates to power dynamics. These complexities had no chance of being distilled in 140 characters or communicated in clickbait headlines.

Regardless, in the court of public opinion, the punishment doled out was about the same, regardless of the crime. Public shaming, cancellation, and crucifixion.

But most importantly, unlike Weinstein, not all of the accused received a trial in an actual court. For some of the real victims, a court case was not a possibility. There was no trail of evidence after so many years or a relevant statute of limitations had expired. Newspaper headlines were all they had.

In the court of public opinion, this meant that some innocent individuals—men, in particular—could lose their careers and reputations with a single tweet, even if they'd committed no crime at all.

After all, "Believe All Women" was the feverish slogan.

Me Too empowered those who had felt powerless and held the feet of the guilty to the fire, but it also obliterated the lives of some innocent people as well. It questioned whether our legal system's concept of "innocent until proven guilty" should extend to our social and moral judgments as well. There were no easy answers to be found.

In this context, a crowdsourced Google spreadsheet surfaced. Its name? Shitty Media Men. It was a collection of anonymous rumors and accusations of sexual misconduct by over seventy men in the media industry. Their purported crimes ranged from being creepy to committing rape. The document served as a whisper network of sorts, a way to semi-privately warn other women in the industry—but it soon became public. This list, which may have been intended to help warn women, effectively became a blacklist, ruining the lives of those on it based entirely on anonymous allegations.

One of the people named was Stephen Elliott, novelist, memoir author (*The Adderall Diaries*), filmmaker, and founder of the online literary magazine *The Rumpus*. His alleged crime: Rape. His accuser? Anonymous.

Now, at this point, it's easy to recoil in disgust. After all, rape is a pretty heinous crime.

And yet, let us for a moment consider the evidence presented: none. But let's rewind for now.

Elliott, who had considered himself a far-left feminist, thought he was doing everything to be "good." *The Rumpus*, which he served as the editor-in-chief of, was extremely liberal and intentionally diverse. Elliott claims credit for discovering literary figures like Cheryl Strayed (*Wild*) and Roxane Gay (*Bad Feminist*) and giving them a platform. Under Elliott's leadership, the publication held monthly events and made sure to always include women and people of color. "We were just trying to be good and these were the things we thought we were supposed to do."

Elliott was deeply political then, especially concerned with prison reform and sex worker rights—having been a sex worker himself. He raised a lot of funds for progressive candidates. "I really did my part," he states. But none of that meant anything once his name appeared on the Shitty Media Men list. "None of the things I had done for these people and for this side of the spectrum [mattered], you know? When people came after me, nobody cared."

As liberal as he was politically, though, Elliott is quick to point out that he had no radical intentions of smashing the state. He was a realist who had studied history in college and, having spent some time learning about revolutions, he was opposed to them. "I felt that revolution is a choice of the unknown over the known, and it's usually a really bad choice. You usually end up with not what you want."

Elliott was living in Los Angeles, trying to make it work as a screenwriter and break into television, when someone brought up the Shitty Media Men list to him over breakfast. He immediately went home, found the list online, and saw that he was being accused of multiple rapes. "Nobody's going to believe that," he thought. In a way, he felt relieved. "It was so obviously a malicious lie. I don't have penetrative sex with women; it's not my sexuality." In fact, Elliott has been quite open about his sexuality, having written about it extensively.

"A lot of people, if they get accused of rape, they might wonder if it's someone who had interpreted or remembered the experience differently. I didn't have those questions because I had not had sex with anybody in a way that could even come close to it, so I knew that it was an intentional lie." Besides, he also knew that he had never had sex with anybody who works in media.

Elliott knew he was innocent, but what about everyone else?

"It was all very surprising," recalls Elliott. A friend publicly distanced herself, saying, "He helped me get my first novel published, and that blinded me to what a monster he was." At least twelve others he'd helped said similar things. People who were in his will denounced him publicly. People with whom he'd been close friends for years. He was essentially excommunicated from his tribe.

"Not every cancellation involves being abandoned by your tribe, but when you are, you learn things about humanity and human nature that you could not learn in any other way."

You learn about how people function, the forces that come into play, and what people are capable of justifying. "In the name of being a good person, people will do the most awful things because they think it makes them good."

You learn how rare it is that people have principles, integrity, and bravery. "It's such a strange thing. When a mob is going in a direction, it's completely intoxicating, and for the people who stand in the middle of that mob, with their tribe, and watch their people going in one direction, and for them to stand still and face the other direction and not get pulled along . . . that is so rare. It's unbelievable."

The number of people whom Elliott had helped within the literary community over the years is high. The number of people who had the courage to defend him publicly: zero. "It's literally zero." This, despite there being a group of people who had reached out to him to let him know they knew the accusations were baseless.

There's a part of Elliott that sympathizes with those unwilling to stick their necks out—to avoid ruining their careers by defending him. "If you didn't say anything, we're fine," he says. "I literally swear to god, I hold no resentment at all to anybody who didn't publicly defend me." His bar of expectations has been set very low: "All you have to do is not say anything." Some of the people who didn't have the courage to defend him have even apologized, to which he'd respond: "You're fine. I have enough people who attacked me publicly to be angry at that I can't waste energy being upset with people who didn't publicly take the position that I wanted people to take."

In the meantime, the list and Elliott's presence on it garnered massive media attention. It was in just about every newspaper, and everyone in the literary world was talking about it nonstop. Elliott's publisher even put out a statement defending the list full of anonymous accusations.

Elliott felt as though there was something deeply tribal about the attacks on him. He watched as close friends got sucked into making hateful comments about him on social media. They wanted to be part of a movement, and that movement was called, Elliott says, "Destroy Stephen Elliott." One such friend had borrowed money just a few weeks earlier. Six months later, she reached out to Elliott for help as if nothing had ever happened. When he brought up her actions—that she had piled on him with the rest of the mob—she acted confused. She claimed not to remember any of it.

"The mob mentality," he explains, "is determinative to human history. Mobs determine all of human history." He cites something he'd written about the Rwandan genocide and the look the Hutus had when they were out killing the Tutsis. "They had this look in their eyes like they were on drugs or something. That's the mob. When you are in the midst of a mob, it's so intoxicating you can literally forget that you were there—that you did or said anything." You're just that swept up in it.

"There's probably nothing more human than the mob," says Elliott. "It's hardwired into us as human beings, and it will always be with us."

Of course, the daily headlines during the Me Too movement made it easy to get confused. The situation was complicated. Some of the accusations were particularly vile and also rather believable. Some of those accused just *sounded* so guilty. It was easy to demand that those abusers and rapists get taken to court, but in other cases, the crime wasn't always so obvious. Often, there simply wasn't enough evidence to make a case—if there was any evidence at all. They were classic he said/she said situations, or even he said/anonymous said ones.

Because all the cases were lumped together in the public imagination, though, it was easy to convict in the court of public opinion. "You've got to assume innocence," insists Elliott. "There's no other way. I mean, it's imperfect and you're going to end up assuming somebody is innocent that isn't, but unless you have more information and there's an anonymously circulating accusation, you just have to assume innocence. And you have to act as if they're innocent. You can't deny them opportunity. You can't say, 'I'm not going to be around that person because it might look bad for me.'"

He cites Blackstone's ratio, which was famously echoed by Benjamin Franklin: "It is better 100 guilty Persons should escape than one innocent Person should suffer." It's one of the foundational ideas of this country, notes Elliott. "And you either subscribe to that or you don't."

Elliott, who grew up in group homes, has long understood this. What's helpful to understand about him is that long before the list, he was already deeply involved in prison reform—working to ensure that children aren't tried as adults, calling for the decriminalization of sex work, and pushing for the prison system to be less punitive. He even helped get someone out of juvenile jail who had been convicted as a child. His activism didn't begin when he was falsely accused. He has held these beliefs and has been fighting for these ideas for a long time.

"But, you know, ultimately, what I really learned through this whole process is the importance of principle. Principles matter, and you have to hold to them no matter what—because if you don't—then everything starts to erode. And soon, you're in a place with no morality whatsoever."

Elliott rejects the idea that things can be so bad or important that it is acceptable to put principles on hold for a while—because we have to fix this *thing*. For example, the notion that some level of collateral damage is acceptable in order to even the playing field between men and women, or correct some injustice, is absurd. It's never okay to ruin innocent people with false accusations in the name of some greater good. Once what needs to be corrected is right again, you can't just go back to assuming innocence as if nothing happened—as if you haven't lost something of your own. That's not how it works.

"That way of thinking takes you down a path you can't get back from. Once you start being unjust and start sacrificing your principles, you will quickly arrive at a place where you have no principles." Then everything you do becomes about tribalism, narcissism, greed, and power, he maintains. "Without principles, the whole house collapses."

The innocent-until-proven-guilty idea is a foundational principle. "I think people will find that the entire American experiment won't stand up without that principle; it just won't work."

Still, there are many people who might stand by this important guiding principle when it comes to the judicial system but will quickly abandon it when it comes to social situations.

"People will very quickly sacrifice their principles when their tribe decides it's time. The mob is an incredibly powerful force, and we will find ways to agree with our tribe, even when it goes against our principles."

If you were a white person of high morals living in the American South in the time of slavery and you were not an avid contrarian with a strong attachment to your principles, he insists, "I guarantee you would have found a way to defend slavery. That's just the way it is. Either you're a person who stands by principles, or you will find a way to defend what your people are doing, and that's what most people do."

That's why the people in power, those making the rules, in particular, have to stand by these higher principles—because the average person won't.

And yes, sometimes that means that guilty people go free. "But the opposite of that is actually much worse, innocent people go to jail." And when accusations are anonymous, "then you're really incentivizing a false accusation."

Not all of Me Too was bad, he fully acknowledges. It drew attention to an existing issue. It opened the floodgates to certain conversations. But what started as a movement based on creating awareness eventually turned into a mob focused on punishment, if not revenge, against often indiscriminate targets. "There's a moment in every movement where it will become irrational. The moment it becomes irrational and people are finding reasons to support it—it's a mob."

Mobs aren't necessarily entirely bad, though. One can harness the power of the mob to make massive changes. But you've got precious little time because the mob will eventually run out of steam. "The French Revolution kept going and going until it burned itself out, and then

Napoleon just came in and took what was left."

When Elliott was taken down by the mob, his entire life changed. For about a year, he didn't really talk to anyone. He stopped going outside. He didn't even watch TV; he just read books for fifteen months. He went into hibernation.

He felt . . . nothing.

Then, about a year and a half in, he got really angry.

"You know, people who are mobbed will never forget the things their friends did during that time, but the people participating in the mob won't remember it a day or two later."

He's particularly critical of the literary community: "It's a place of conformity . . . you'll be hard-pressed to find a community with less integrity than the literary community because, by definition, they've sold out everything to their ambition. They've decided that attention and success in this world is more important than money—because you don't even do it for the money. It's a zero-sum game, there's very little to go around . . . and you don't even notice that you're shedding yourself to be in this world, you know?"

Everyone in the literary world also tends to share the same political views and go along with whatever is popular among that tribe. "You have to compromise yourself so many times to exist as a short story writer or as a poet that you don't even notice small compromises you make along the way." One might imagine that writers would have more integrity since they are living the life of an artist, but Elliott is quick to point out that there are very few "outsider" artists.

Unlike members of the literary community, a good number of people in the sex worker community publicly defended Elliott—despite the cost of doing so. "The sex worker community clearly just had much more integrity than the literary community." Meanwhile, the literary community was trying to bend itself into a pretzel to defend an anonymous list. "It's indefensible. A list full of anonymous accusations is simply indefensible." Elliott was so convinced of that point that he sued the list's creator. That's when he truly awakened the mob's ire.

The "Shitty Media Men List" was, in many ways, a foundational document for the Me Too movement. To challenge it by asserting that there are innocent people on that list falsely accused of things like rape would cast doubt on the whole project. Was Me Too a massive overreaction? Did we let our principles go because we thought this was so important? Elliott thinks so. "It just calls everything into question, and so people are inspired to kind of circle the wagons and defend this precious thing—which is not something that can be actually defended by a moral, logical, or rational person."

Before he brought the lawsuit against the list's creator, Elliott had already been uninvited from all things in the literary world and subject to online mobbing. But when he filed the lawsuit, he began to experience anger, outrage, and shunning on a whole new level. He moved to New Orleans, where he didn't even know anybody, and he thought nobody would recognize him, and yet his house *still* got vandalized. Then, his car got spray-painted with a single word: "rapist."

"Even in a city where I don't know people, I still have to deal with this kind of stuff."

Even today, he doesn't think he'll ever be able to make a living as a writer again. Losing his agent, his publisher, and his opportunities was hard, he says. "But more than that," he notes, "I lost my tribe. I lost so many close friends. So many people that I thought were really important people in my life."

That was harder than anything else for Elliott. "Anybody that tells you otherwise is not being honest, or they have not been canceled in the worst possible way." Getting kicked out of your tribe is particularly difficult because you lose your entire identity. As Elliott learned, you no longer know who you really are.

The process came in steps. As Elliott explains, at first, you argue your case and try to see things from their end. Then, you start making excuses for them—because they are your friends. But ultimately, you begin to question everything. Have your beliefs been wrong? If you thought you were doing everything right, what else have you been wrong about? If you've spent all this time aligning with people who have rejected you, where does it leave you? "You have no idea how earth-shattering it is to have your identity completely stripped."

Still, despite becoming even more of an outcast, he does not regret the lawsuit. There's no version of him that doesn't file it. It's simply who he is and has always been. "I couldn't live with myself never filing that lawsuit. I'm not the only person falsely accused on that list—that list is a false accusation machine."

When Elliott filed the lawsuit, a few others on it reached out to him. Finally, they had someone to commiserate with. They'd begin by giving him a deep and detailed recollection of what their case was, what they did or didn't do, and what was false or exaggerated. He'd stop them. "I don't care. I know that no matter what you did, if you did anything, you have suffered more than your crime entails." That suffering includes massive public humiliation and the loss of family, friends, and livelihood. "Every single one of them would talk to me about suicidal ideation and how they had gone through a period of where they could only think about suicide all day long."

After the anger came, Elliott eventually started to make an effort to return to some semblance of normalcy. He began to go to outside. He'd visit a coffee shop. He went to meetings. He eventually began to go to the gym to feel better due to complications with multiple sclerosis. He started meeting new people.

A bit less than two years after his cancellation, Elliott came out the other side and suddenly knew exactly how he felt about it. It wasn't complicated anymore. If somebody had asked him to explain it to them, it would take no time at all. "That's when you're ready to go back on with your life."

Yet, the worry that someone can easily google his name always looms. It has resulted in some awkward moments. "But I'm kind of at the point now where if you're okay with anonymous lists . . . I don't want to know you."

The experience has certainly transformed Elliott. He's shed his deeply political shell and tries to be less and less political every day. "I have fewer and fewer beliefs." Fewer things to argue over. He doesn't care anymore about the politics of the people he spends time with. Instead, he looks at basics: Are you a good person? Do you volunteer? Do you help your friends move? Are you there for your friends? Will you visit them in the hospital? Do you have principles or are you willing to betray them to get power because you're so certain that you're right? That's what's important; those are the real questions. The rest seems meaningless now.

"We must cultivate our own garden," he says, quoting Voltaire. But for Elliot, that is just the first step: we should also share our gardens with those we love and care for. "I care about my family. I care about the people I'm around. I want to keep my side of the street clean. I'm not really worried about what's going on in the world. I'll leave that for the kids." There's a lot of freedom to be found in getting canceled. You can say or do anything you want. But there are certain things Elliott will likely never get to do again—like land a book deal with a Big Five publisher.

The defamation lawsuit that Elliott filed against the creator of the "Shitty Media Men List" was finally settled in March 2023—with a six-figure amount in his favor. In an emailed statement to the *Washington Post*, he admitted that "there's some closure here" and that there's "enough money that it's basically an admission of guilt, and it feels like a victory." He felt that filing the lawsuit was a moral obligation.

But, while there's some sort of "win" in his story, it will never rewind the destruction of his reputation and his career or the pain that he's experienced. Of the media outlets that covered the initial accusations against him, far fewer covered the settlement.

This is the unfortunate reality of our current environment. Today's media has far more important stories to cover, like those involving the next person to be tried in the court of public opinion. Given the sheer volume of social media pile-ons and online mobs today, Elliott concludes, "We're reaching some kind of a critical mass where everybody knows somebody who has been falsely accused of something."

We can only hope that this means the tide is finally shifting and that we as a public will no longer reflexively condemn and punish based on anonymous accusations.

## Notes

As many who have been accused of a crime and later been exonerated discover, the initial accusation receives far more interest and coverage than the later vindication. This was certainly the case for Elliott. When his lawsuit was settled, there were far fewer media articles than when his life was shattered by an anonymous accusation. But at least a few publications did make a note of the outcome, including Jessica Testa, "'Media Men' Lawsuit Ends in a Settlement," *New York Times*, March 6, 2023, www.nytimes.com/2023/03/06/style/media-men-list-settlement-moira-donegan.html; and Jonathan Kay, "The 'Shitty Media Men' Legal Saga Comes to a Close," *Quillette*, March 9, 2023, quillette.com/2023/03/09/the-shtty-media-men-legal-saga-comes-to-a-close.

There's also an interesting piece that examines libel and legal implications when it comes to Section 230 of the U.S. Communications Decency Act: Eriq Gardner, "Evidence Destruction Warrants 'Shitty Media Men' Trial, Says Writer," *Hollywood Reporter*, June 3, 2021, www.hollywoodreporter.com/news/general-news/shitty-media-men-creator-1234962535.

In light of a group of anonymous students at the University of Washington launching a website called "Make Them Scared," which invites and publishes anonymous accusations of harassment, abuse, and rape against named individuals, journalist Katie Herzog revisited the Shitty Media Men list and Elliott's experiences on it in a piece for *The Stranger*: "Anonymous UW Students Publish Rape Accusations Online. What

Could Go Wrong?" *Stranger*, October 9, 2018, www.thestranger.com/news/2018/10/09/33615110/anonymous-uw-students-publish-rape-accusations-online-what-could-go-wrong. The creators of the website told the school's student newspaper, *The Daily*, that they "want to give victims a sense of justice and rest that other avenues deny them. Although catharsis for victims is part of it, we aren't publishing the names for the sake of that alone. We also want the list to serve as a deterrent for future perpetrators and as a resource for potential victims to consult for their own safety." Notably, the paper's editorial board stated the following when breaking the news about the existence of the student-created website: "The editorial board cannot justify the actions of the list's creators . . . It completely circumvents due process and trivializes the seriousness with which accusations ought to be received. It ends up lending more credit to the argument that even truthful accusations should be viewed with suspicion and as part of a vengeful agenda, not one that seeks justice." For their full statement, see "Student-Created Website Allowing for Anonymous Sexual Assault Allegations Vulnerable to Defamation Charges," *Daily*, October 1, 2018 (updated August 12, 2021), www.dailyuw.com/news/article_dd14bf34-c5f6-11e8-a705-cf14683d53a3.html.

By the time news of the site broke, several names had already been removed from the anonymous list. As the student paper reported, the site moderators "acknowledged that they are aware publishing false accusations makes them vulnerable to libel or defamation lawsuits," demonstrating that "deterrence" works both ways. As Elliott himself noted, this type of deterrence is a moral obligation—and remains effective only if the innocently accused continue to fight back through legal means.

# 5 Speak Truth in the Face of Danger

## The Lessons of Peter Boghossian

*I don't want to be a punk. I'm not going to be pushed around by third-grade ideologues. And I also think that as long as you're willing to change your mind about something—that should be the North Star of any kind of intellectual endeavor.*

—*Peter Boghossian*

While an assistant professor of philosophy at Portland State University, Peter Boghossian was involved in the "Grievance Studies Affair" (also known as the Sokal Squared scandal) with James Lindsay and Helen Pluckrose. The trio published hoax papers in academic journals in order to call attention to the lack of rigor and ideological corruption in fields like gender studies. This resulted in Portland State launching a research misconduct investigation against Boghossian and, eventually, Boghossian's resignation from the school. Even without the misconduct investigation, it wouldn't be a stretch to say that his departure from the school was inevitable.

Known for challenging orthodoxies, Boghossian had a history of speaking out in favor of more diversity of thought on campus and inviting speakers that some deemed controversial—much to the chagrin of many Portland State administrators and colleagues. As Boghossian shared in his now-infamous resignation letter, in addition to "exploring classic philosophers and traditional texts," he had invited guest lecturers ranging from "Flat-Earthers to Christian apologists to global climate skeptics to Occupy Wall Street advocates." He didn't invite these speakers because he agreed with their worldviews. Rather, as he noted, he invited them "primarily" because he *didn't* agree with them. "From those messy and difficult conversations, I've seen the best of what our students can achieve: questioning beliefs while respecting believers; staying even-tempered in challenging circumstances; and even changing their minds," he wrote.

But over time, Boghossian found that this kind of intellectual exploration became impossible at a school like Portland State. The university had "transformed a bastion of free inquiry" into a "Social Justice factory whose only inputs were race, gender, and victimhood and whose only outputs were grievance and division." According to Boghossian, students weren't being taught to think for themselves; they were "being trained to mimic the moral certainty of ideologues" and have abdicated their pursuit of truth only to replace it with "intolerance for divergent beliefs and opinions." This made open and honest discussion impossible. To Boghossian, institutions like PSU have become the definition of illiberalism.

And the more he spoke out about the issues he was seeing, the more retaliation he faced—from the university, faculty, and students.

But Boghossian didn't exactly set out to be controversial. Growing up, he never thought of himself as particularly opinionated. Even today, he describes himself as "average with a tinge of iconoclasm" but not particularly opinionated (even if many of his fans and detractors might disagree with this particular self-assessment).

As an assistant professor at Portland State, Boghossian enjoyed the community feel of the urban campus. He felt at home with the many working-class people who attended the university, having grown up around working-class families. (His father was a civil engineer, and his mother managed medical offices.) Boghossian was a popular instructor who avoided formal airs and had students refer to him as Pete or Peter rather than by Prof. Boghossian or Dr. Boghossian.

At some point, though, the environment around him started to shift. Boghossian began to receive a constant stream of emails from university administrators and his department about diversity, equity, and inclusion—to the exclusion of all else. "It was incessant; it made you take notice." So, curious, he went to the meetings. "I was totally blown away. There was no diversity on the diversity panel. The panel was made up of different faculty members, but they all had the same opinions, and they were identical opinions."

Perhaps naively, Boghossian thought that diversity had referred to physical and intellectual differences, as well as a variety of beliefs. "I didn't understand at the time that diversity meant ideological homogeneity."

This was the beginning of a long and uncomfortable journey for him at Portland State. "At the time, I wasn't questioning or challenging," insists Boghossian. "I was just trying to understand what was going on." And yet, when he posed a question about microaggressions—asking what the evidence for it was—a colleague told him that asking for evidence for microaggressions is, in fact, a microaggression itself.

When he was asked by a student if race was a social construct or a valid biological category, he responded that he is an educator and a philosopher, not a biologist—and that it was best to ask this question to someone in the biology department. The student reported him. Boghossian was constantly investigated and brought in for questioning. "It was a carnival of madness," he recalls.

In his class on New Atheism, he'd teach about the work of the "Four Horsemen"—Richard Dawkins, Sam Harris, Christopher Hitchens, and Daniel Dennett—all authors of bestselling books that were critical of religion. Some students were upset that these thinkers, who were largely responsible for the growing interest in atheism in the mid-2000s and early 2010s, were all male and that none were gay or trans. So they complained.

One day, Boghossian asked the university's chief diversity officer to explain diversity to him—he even offered to take him out to lunch. The officer reported Boghossian, too.

What was it about Boghossian simply asking questions that caused such distress? "I think the very fact that you asked the questions means you haven't been through a catechism—it means that you're not already a believer," he explains. "I think that deep down, many of these people realize that there's simply no evidence, and when there's no evidence for the thing you believe, you must invent your own epistemology. So they invent things like standpoint theory, their lived experience trumping everything, all this nonsense. And I think asking those questions was fundamentally threatening to them."

These days, however, Boghossian is no longer just asking questions and curiously trying to figure things out. He's actively on the offensive, trying to dismantle what he perceives to be an ideology that has done massive damage to both individuals and institutions.

Boghossian had learned something very important from the New Atheist movement. "I learned that if you can delegitimize canonical texts, you can decrease the confidence people have in their beliefs." That's what led to the Grievance Studies Affair—the hoax papers that made worldwide media headlines for passing peer review and getting published in academic journals despite being completely ridiculous or morally abhorrent. Among them was a paper about canine rape culture in dog parks, which was accepted by the feminist geography journal *Gender, Place and Culture*. In fact, seven out of the twenty of the papers submitted had been accepted by journals when their hoax was exposed in the *Wall Street Journal*. "Everybody lost their minds," recalls Boghossian. The success of getting a paper in one of the best journals in gender studies showed that the body of work upon which these beliefs are formed is just "make-believe land." And yet, somehow, the rational mind is overridden. Why?

"I think when you cull intellectual diversity, you're left in a monoculture. And when you have nobody to challenge your beliefs, you increase
the confidence in those beliefs you have. That's part of it."

The rational mind on U.S. campuses is also being overridden, at
least in part, by "white guilt"—professing privilege and atoning for past
wrongs has become almost a ritual for many white professors in the
United States. Boghossian, however, never fell into it. He feels zero guilt
for anything that may have occurred in the past. All of his grandparents
are immigrants who came to the United States on a boat, he explains.
The Armenian ones narrowly escaped genocide. His grandmother hid
in an attic in a Turkish family's house for two years. His grandfather
worked on a steamship, shoveled coal, and got lung cancer. None of his
ancestors were slaveholders. Why should he feel guilty about the past?
And yet, it has become morally fashionable to claim that feeling.

At first, Boghossian was relatively indifferent to the endless stream
of personal attacks against him on social media, from the institution,
and even on the streets. "That's part of the struggle of the modern age, to
figure out whose voice does not matter." Why should he care about what
someone thinks if he doesn't even know them—if they haven't earned
his respect? "Why should I give their voice or provocation credence?"
He chooses instead to rely on counsel from people he respects, people
like evolutionary biologist Richard Dawkins and *Skeptic* magazine publisher Michael Shermer—whom he counts as friends and who model the
type of fearless intellectual behavior Boghossian admires, a willingness
to modify beliefs based on evidence.

"I don't want to be a punk. I'm not going to be pushed around by
third-grade ideologues. And I also think that as long as you're willing
to change your mind about something—that should be the North Star
of any kind of intellectual endeavor." Too often, though, when someone
sincerely asks something that questions someone else's belief, if they are
unable to answer that question, they lash out. "They feel exposed," says
Boghossian. It can cause them to feel backed into a corner. As a result,

they act out of fear—they begin to attack the person who posed the question with personal slander or screams or claims that they are offended.

Perhaps in that way, instead of providing answers to Boghossian's questions, the Office of Diversity, Equity, and Inclusion chose a campaign of endless investigations, while those who opposed the holes he poked in their ideologies submitted Title IX complaints instead of engaging in honest, open dialogue.

"We give far too much credence to people who say they're offended," says Boghossian. "Why shouldn't some people be offended? What if you went through a whole life and you had some crazy belief, and you were never offended? Sometimes, people should be offended. But here's the dividing line: If somebody criticizes an immutable characteristic ... if somebody levels a criticism against you because of something you can't change, what's the point in criticizing it?"

Boghossian finds it bizarre that we seem to buy into the ideas of a "deranged minority of people" who are pushing political and moral agendas. And, he insists, "the longer it takes people to say 'fuck you, I don't accept that,' the worse it's going to be.'" It's one thing to be reflective about something that has some merit, but when the accusation being foisted on you is something you don't subscribe to, why give credence to the criticisms?

Still, there's no denying that people are terrified to push back, let alone say "fuck you." According to Boghossian, it's either because they are hyper-attuned to the sensitivities of others or it's because they believe that their own personal situation will become worse if they fight back. But, he insists, it's exactly the opposite. "People will respect you. They respect strength and integrity. They don't respect weakness, and these people are vultures that pick through the misfortunes of those on the other side of the ideological divide."

There are now countless examples of people who have lost their jobs and reputations to the mob. When accusations are made publicly, those who don't know the person involved often don't know what to believe. Those who have the power to defend the accused too often stay silent. "They don't speak because they are fucking cowards," says Boghossian, refusing to mince words, "They are."

Even so, it's hard to deny that careers and lives have been destroyed by nothing more than accusations, no matter how hard the accused might push back against them. What advice might he have for them? After all, Boghossian fought back, but he still gave up something in the process: his job.

"I think that there are many individuals who are accused and don't have access to the right tools. They don't have access to the magic words: 'Fuck you.' You don't need any special gimmicks. Just 'fuck you.' That's all you need to say. There's literally nothing else. But people think that if they say they're sorry, they will be redeemed. They will be forgiven if they just apologize. But there's no forgiveness. There's no forgiving of people in the new religion. The new religion doesn't forgive people."

It can't continue this way indefinitely, insists Boghossian. Eventually, you're going to get too many people who have run afoul of the dominant moral orthodoxy. "You just cannot run a society in which literally everybody is canceled. It's just not possible." It's bound to collapse on itself. The question is: How long will it take?

For Boghossian, the end of this "moral orthodoxy" can't come soon enough, but in the meantime, it's hard to imagine that his experiences haven't left some sort of traumatic footprint on him. Aside from the endless investigations by the university, for example, he's been falsely accused of beating his wife and kids. Swastikas with his name under them appeared in the bathroom near the philosophy department and then on his office door, accompanied by bags of feces. He's been subjected to physical threats, had a bottle thrown at him, was spit on, and more. It was not lost on him that the university remained notably silent when it came to addressing the perpetrators.

"You get used to it, you know?" he says before correcting himself:

"Well, not really." He mentions that at least no one has ever broken into his house. In the same breath, he admits that he has several guns. "I'm ready."

In his resignation letter, Boghossian wrote about the Title IX investigations against him: "With Title IX investigations, there is no due process, so I didn't have access to the particular accusations, the ability to confront my accuser, and I had no opportunity to defend myself. Finally, the results of the investigation were revealed in December 2017. Here are the last two sentences of the report: 'Global Diversity & Inclusion finds there is insufficient evidence that Boghossian violated PSU's Prohibited Discrimination & Harassment policy. GDI recommends Boghossian receive coaching.'" He received no apology.

Remaining silent for Boghossian was never an option, though. It's not just about courage. "A lot of people do [stay silent]," he says, "and they've compromised their integrity, creating a situation that's almost more difficult for them to get out of. But I think, in my case, it was a little different. I literally teach critical thinking and moral reasoning for a living, so I think there was more of an onus on me to speak up against something that was crazy."

When people remain silent, bad ideas are allowed to spread. "You have to call them out. You have to be a bug spray for bad ideas." So, the idea of staying silent never even occurred to Boghossian. "Why would it occur to me? The ideas aren't true, so why should anybody stay silent in the face of something that's so blatantly fallacious?"

Asked whether it might be understandable for someone to remain silent to avoid trouble, Boghossian replies, "Maybe, but then you'd have no moral standard. You'd have no integrity. You'd be a person who had collapsed from the inside. To be blown around by the winds of whatever the culture told you."

There are so many people walking around, ashamed, because they know what the truth is, but they are too afraid to utter it. Those same people will whisper to people like Boghossian and thank him for what he's doing or write emails—but they won't speak out. "This is the human condition," he says. "It's a mimetic competition of ideas. There are always ideas that float around in a given society, and the way that we deal with those ideas tells us about ourselves."

There's something about a person who speaks truth in the face of danger, a person who retains their integrity—that nothing can harm them. They become bulletproof, argues Boghossian. "I feel bulletproof, too. In terms of my own integrity, I'm bulletproof." Given some of the threats he's received, however, he's quick to jokingly add that he's not bulletproof at all when it comes to actual bullets.

"I mean, look, you only have one life. What kind of life do you want to live? You don't want to be the person who laments or regrets or [lives in] fear. Why do you fear people whose voices don't even matter [to you]?"

The last few sentences in Boghossian's resignation letter reads: "For ten years, I have taught my students the importance of living by your principles. One of mine is to defend our system of liberal education from those who seek to destroy it. Who would I be if I didn't?"

## Notes

Boghossian's resignation letter, "My University Sacrificed Ideas for Ideology. So Today I Quit," which was published by The Free Press on September 8, 2021, made headlines worldwide. You can read it on their website: www.thefp.com/p/my-university-sacrificed-ideas-for

Documentary filmmaker Mike Nayna managed to capture the entire Grievance Studies Affair from its inception to its discovery. The footage, which featured its participants—Peter Boghossian, James Lindsay, and Helen Pluckrose—was released on June 20, 2023, as a four-part documentary titled The Reformers on Nayna's Substack: www.michaelnayna.com/p/the-reformers-recommended-viewing?sd=pf.

Boghossian has his own YouTube Channel where he posts his (sometimes heated) Spectrum Street Epistemology videos and interviews with people like Glenn Loury, John McWhorter, Richard Dawkin, Michael Shermer, Helen Joyce, and Kellie-Jay Keen (Posie Parker) in which they often discuss "controversial" topics: www.youtube.com/drpeterboghossian.

He also writes on his Substack at boghossian.substack.com/ and posts on X @peterboghossian.

# 6  Be Open-Minded, but Don't Be Gaslit

## The Lessons of Christopher Wells

*I remember starting to question: Am I actually an evil person?*
*All these people are telling me my beliefs are evil.*

—*Christopher Wells*

The mob doesn't discriminate by age. Often, students are the easiest and most vulnerable targets. Born and bred in Arlington, Virginia, Christopher Wells is a dual U.S. and Canadian citizen. Politics has always had a strong presence in his life—with both parents being journalists. "Writers," he quickly corrects himself. "Journalist has become a bit of a slur." Like many writers, they are also bleeding-heart progressives.

Taking after his parents, Wells has always been outspoken. His nickname in high school was the "county socialist," where he was the lone "Bernie bro" and president of the Young Democrats. "I was very far to the left, but you could think of me as a class-based leftist," he clarifies. He wasn't so concerned with social justice to the extent that it was becoming a dogma, but he was rather politically incorrect for a straight white male. "I still am," he admits.

But over time, his views gradually evolved. "It was maybe a two-year process to come out of the closet as heterodox to some extent," he says.

93

During his senior year, Wells started eating lunch with a guy whom he describes as the Ben Shapiro of the school. As the lone socialist agitator at the school, Wells didn't have many options for lunch companions. The Shapiro-alike had to do. Unsurprisingly, they would butt heads. "But this guy is so, so bright, and through discourse, he put me in my place every time," admits Wells. "I wasn't willing to question my overall politics, but he'd get me on issues like 'white privilege.'"

One time, after a particularly heated argument, Wells told him that he was over it: "I'm having a terrible day—you win." What caught him off guard was his nemesis's response: He told Wells that he was very sorry for how he was feeling and that he was there for him if he wanted to talk about things other than politics. "The way he reacted, I had my first moment of 'Oh, my God, conservatives are not evil people.' And we just end up being best friends."

By the end of twelfth grade, as a result of the amazing and challenging conversations he was having with his now friend, Wells began to question all of his politics. He also started missing Young Democrats meetings. "And it's not even that my politics have shifted," he says. "I'm just kind of sick of partisanship at this point. So we kind of pull each other toward the center."

In time, Wells discovered some of the thinkers in the so-called Intellectual Dark Web (IDW), people like Eric and Bret Weinstein, as well as Jordan Peterson. "It was this weird cognitive dissonance where I was like, yeah, I'm still progressive, but everything that they're saying is true." He became aware of just how many terrible but infectious ideas had taken hold in society that are inherently not doing the positive things that people have convinced themselves that they are.

Today, Wells studies in Canada's University of British Columbia (UBC), majoring in classical studies in the hopes of pursuing law so that he can go into First Amendment litigation. Many of his classmates are so far to the left that they define themselves as classical Marxists. Wells sees the fundamental fiscal and structural issues that they are concerned about, but he notes, "People totally forget how just one bad social idea can totally tear apart a society." He asks, "To what extent can you claim that [a] country is inherently evil and irreconcilable from the inside and still make any form of progress?"

At the University of British Columbia, Wells has found himself pretty isolated. Unlike in high school, this sense of isolation comes not just from students but also from professors. In an African Studies course, for example, he was told not to comment on a particular subject because he's a straight white male. He didn't like being told not to speak in class, so he made a provocative Instagram post about it. Next thing he knew, his whole residence was after him. The girl he was seeing came to his door in tears.

Six months later, at the height of Black Lives Matter, he posted a heartfelt message asking people to remember not to hate each other regardless of beliefs. That's when a fellow student at the university who wrote for a large media publication posted something to her 14,000 followers in which she threatened others not to be friends with Wells. Wells had just moved in with housemates of very pro-BLM far leftists. Needless to say, when people on social media started saying, "We know which of you live with racist reactionaries," they turned against him. With an online army dispatched against him in the middle of COVID-19 lockdowns, Well says, "I kind of went crazy . . . I was smoking pot all day." At that point, he felt, for lack of a better word, gaslit. "I remember starting to question: Am I actually an evil person? All these people are telling me my beliefs are evil."

In retrospect, Wells thinks that he shoulders some of the blame for how he handled things. "I look at how much unnecessary suffering I've caused for myself," he admits. His marijuana addiction didn't help matters either. But more so, he regrets how he carried himself at times. "It kind of comes down to . . . You can have all these principles, but it doesn't mean anything until you can practice them."

Wells says that sometimes you're in a position when you know that people will disagree with you, but you must dissent anyway and be willing to pay the price. "But more than anything, you have to be comfortable with how you went about it. So, I much prefer the MLK to the Malcolm X, the Coleman Hughes to the Jordan Peterson. So now when I do dissent, I'm not only very careful, but I try to appeal to empathy rather than any form of righteousness."

What's particularly disturbing about this movement toward this intolerance of ideas, though, says Wells, is that there's no one figurehead. "It's interesting because with these movements, particularly McCarthyism, there was just one person you had to take out, and then the whole movement was over. When McCarthy was done, McCarthyism was done." But when it comes to this dogma, there's no leader. It's a game of Whack-a-Mole. "You vote out AOC, and Ilhan Omar will come along. It's like a hydra. You cut off the head, and five more pop up. Which is what makes it impossible to legislate against this, and it's frankly a bad idea."

Wells' parents were huge academics. His mother has three Ivy League degrees. His father graduated magna cum laude. "It was just this vigorous place of debate," says Wells, lamenting what once was. "What is most disconcerting to me is how professors are afraid of their own students." He says that a lot of the students and professors go along with the political dogma not so much because they believe in it but because they are afraid or because they just really don't understand the linguistic traps.

"Imagine having the gall to question white privilege or equity or whatever dog whistle you want in the classroom? It is akin to questioning Jesus in a church." Even tenured professors are afraid because no one wants to be hauled in front of an investigatory board, suffer a reputational loss, and go through a closed-door kangaroo court. "Even if you make it out of the session alive, all of your colleagues know that you were brought in front of the DEI board. They don't know why—they just know you've done something bad. It's institutionalized."

Wells points out that the older professors tend to go along because they have no choice. They tend to have more of a Noam Chomsky lens, he says, adding he has yet to have a conservative professor. The new crop of PhDs, on the other hand, are true believers. "Those are the terrifying ones; they've been ideologically vetted." These days, many colleges and universities require that applicants fill out DEI statements in order to be considered for a position.

To ensure a good grade with new professors, Wells admits he has to play the game sometimes. "I've actually had a lot of fun writing incredibly outlandish papers, and it helps me understand the epistemological standpoint of some of these people better." He wrote his English final on a Kipling short story about a man who's being haunted by a ghost. "I essentially wrote that he's being haunted by this ghost because he's implicitly upholding the patriarchy and white supremacy. I had a lot of fun doing that."

Surprisingly, no one caught on—or questioned his analysis. "The more outlandish you can get and still get away with it, the better you'll be marked. The more insane you can push it and seem genuine, the better."

As for his fellow students, Wells says that there appears to be a silent majority. Some of them are scared, and many more just don't understand the issues or cannot be bothered. And, of course, there are those who actively uphold the ideologies and suppression of dissenting views. "Then there's a handful of dissenters who do it very, very occasionally and very strategically." Wells is, of course, one of them. "I used to let it affect my social standing, but I think I do it well enough now that the only people I really put off are the loud minority. But I think most people really don't see the almost cult-like brainwashing."

So what will become of students graduating from a school culture where dissent and questioning things outside a particular narrative is generally discouraged? As Greg Lukianoff and Jonathan Haidt's *The Coddling of the American Mind* demonstrates, the concern goes well beyond questions of free expression and speech; it also negatively impacts mental strength, resiliency, and the ability to deal with hardships and conflicts.

"I think what I really noticed is a generation of people being told exactly what to do," says Wells. "And then when they enter the workplace, and you kind of have to figure it out, they're lost. So it's not just political at that point. It's a weak generation. It's an utterly helpless generation who have been coddled in every sense possible yet are so self-righteous."

As Wells looks at the struggles of past generations who have had to deal with wars, food shortages, and other profound hardships, he can't help by notice that "for whatever reason, my generation thinks we're in the worst of times."

## Notes

Wells was featured in a *New York Post* piece that profiled college students who felt that college campuses had become "increasingly radical, illiberal, and intolerant of dissenting opinions." He told the paper that although he thought of himself as a progressive, he was skeptical of social justice ideology and identity politics because he viewed them as a distraction from class issues and a threat to something he deeply valued: free speech. "When I got to campus, " he explained, "I found the core tenets of social justice are taken as objective truths, not viewpoints that should be vigorously debated. I quickly learned not to write papers going against the established narrative for fear of being marked down." See Rikki Schlott, "Five College Students Speak Out: We're Fed Up with Campus 'Wokeness,'" *New York Post*, January 15, 2022, nypost.com/2022/01/15/five-college-students-speak-out-against-campus-wokeness.

To understand much of what Wells describes, see Greg Lukianoff and Jonathan Haidt, *The Coddling of the American Mind: How Good Intentions and Bad Ideas Are Setting Up a Generation for Failure* (Penguin, 2018).

Wells keeps a low profile these days.

# 7 Know That Friends Will Disappoint You

## The Lessons of Bret Weinstein (Part One)

*People will look back on this moment, and they will look
at those who stood up. You don't want to be one of the people
who made the wrong call.*

—Bret Weinstein

Do you want to live in a manner that's honest to who you are as a person, or are you comfortable walking on eggshells and stifled for the rest of your life? Either way, you're going to pay a price. It's just a matter of choosing what you're willing to pay for and how much.

When evolutionary biologist Bret Weinstein objected to the annual Day of Absence at Washington's Evergreen State College in 2017, there was no doubt that a certain level of courage was involved. Unlike previous years, when students and faculty of color stayed off campus to highlight their contributions, that year's event organizers requested instead that white students and faculty members stay off campus.

Weinstein voiced his opposition on a campus email list. He wrote, "There is a huge difference between a group or coalition deciding to voluntarily absent themselves from a shared space in order to highlight their vital and underappreciated roles (the theme of the Douglas Turner

Ward play *Day of Absence*, as well as the recent Women's Day walkout) and a group encouraging another group to go away. The first is a forceful call to consciousness, which is, of course, crippling to the logic of oppression. The second is a show of force and an act of oppression in and of itself." He added, "On a college campus, one's right to speak—or to be—must never be based on skin color."

The email was widely shared, prompting a flood of threats against him and calls for his firing and making it unsafe for him to remain on campus. Ultimately, this resulted in a $3.85 million lawsuit by Weinstein and Heather Heying, his wife and fellow faculty member at Evergreen, against the college for failing to protect them. Weinstein and Heying alleged that it had "permitted, cultivated, and perpetuated a racially hostile and retaliatory work environment." Ultimately, the suit was settled. Weinstein and Heying received $500,000 in exchange for their resignations from the college.

"One thing that is true is that Heather and I are very close and have been for a very long time . . . [which] made both of us braver in the face of what we were confronted with because, you know, there was never any jeopardy to our whole world," explains Weinstein. "I was raised with the expectation that things might not always be sunny and that it might be necessary to confront evil, and I think it would also have been hard to live with myself if I hadn't stood up and said what I knew full well to be the case."

What is often missed in the coverage of the aftermath of what happened at Evergreen is the fact that both Weinstein and Heying had taught at the college for fourteen and fifteen years, respectively, and had a large community of very dedicated students, many of whom were grateful for the opportunities offered within their professors' classrooms. "The number of people who knew that the way we were both being smeared in public wasn't true was substantial, and many of them were actually willing to stand up and say so—including students of color—who took an even bigger risk than most."

Those who attacked Weinstein had expected that his students would defect and join in on the attacks on him, yet not a single one did. However, that didn't stop protesters from showing up to his classroom demanding that he would either submit to their control or lose his livelihood. Despite his longstanding commitment to the college and his students, the self-appointed justice mob decided that they had the right to determine whether or not he could earn a living or put a roof over his family's head because they saw him as an obstacle in their fight. "That's nonsense," says Weinstein. "You can't run a civilization that way."

Today a recognizable figure, he says that people stop him all the time to talk to him about what happened to him. They frequently invoke the word bravery. It's not entirely wrong, but, he says, "It's not what the experience of it was. When somebody stands up and says: 'This college is riddled with white supremacy, and you're a racist,' the only thing to do is to stand up and say, 'There's not a shred of evidence for what you're saying and here's how I know it to be wrong.'"

Feelings have been weaponized as a way of shutting down discussions and silencing those who say things that might cause certain people to feel aggrieved, regardless of intention. Punishment gets doled out the same. "Again," he insists, "you can't run a civilization that way."

As a Jewish kid growing up in the United States in the 70s and 80s, Weinstein was in contact with an awful lot of people who had experienced the Holocaust directly. And while what's currently happening in the United States or what happened at Evergreen isn't close to being comparable, the lessons about human nature still apply. What Weinstein is observing is a similar pattern that involves the process of dehumanizing groups of people. Jews have frequently been a demonized group since they tend to exist as a minority inside societies—but this "game" works anytime there's a group that can be successfully targeted and is not in a position to defend itself. "There were shifts in the political winds that caused white people, especially white men, to be suspect in liberal circles, which meant that virtually any allegation would be believed."

This process of demonization often goes hand in hand with another feature of humans that has been tragically witnessed time and again throughout history. People often remain silent in the face of the mob and won't stand up for you—even presumed friends. In the case of Evergreen, says Weinstein, the number of people who knew better and should have stood up but didn't was very large. On the positive side, he notes, the number of people that you would not have expected to stand up and continue to speak the truth—despite being bullied, confronted, and shouted down—was also very large: "People will surprise you in both directions."

He adds, "There's a process—it's a painful process—but it's one that people need to be aware of. If you do the right thing, in a circumstance like that, you will lose a lot of people, and you will pick up others. And that is a process of upgrade. Your social environment improves because the quality of people around you goes up."

But it's an unpredictable process. As he acknowledges, some of the people you'll end up losing may surprise you, and it will hurt. "The fact is," he says, "you have to extrapolate and realize that those aren't the people you want to have around you. If it takes a crisis to reveal that somebody that you're counting on can't be counted upon, then so be it."

So what is that quality that allows some to remain silent even as they know harm is being done, whereas others will stick their necks out? "I wish I knew," says Weinstein. "It's almost a willingness to put personal well-being aside, which is a characteristic that is becoming less and less common."

Weinstein believes that the most important things in life require sacrifice or risk: "There's something important about modeling this behavior so that those who have it within them to stand up will."

"We need them to stand up," he says. But given the sometimes-high risks that come with standing up, should we always encourage others to do so? If they ended up losing their job, too, for example, would we not be responsible for their downfall?

The key is honesty and transparency, says Weinstein. "If someone stands up on the basis that someone else has encouraged them to and convinced them that they would be just fine if they do—they've been misled." That would not be right, he says. People shouldn't stand up because they don't think it will be that bad. On the contrary, Weinstein notes, "it should be because [they] know it's worth it and important." Weinstein says, ultimately, it's up to each individual to decide for themselves: "I don't want the responsibility of making that decision for others."

In the Evergreen context, some of the people who stood up for Weinstein faced terrible consequences. But, he says, he doesn't know anyone who stood up and regrets it. "I think everybody who did knows it was the right thing, and I suspect that quite a number of people who failed to stand up have deep regrets and shame."

But just as he and his wife were surprised by who stood up and who didn't, those individuals may have surprised even themselves. "They might have thought they wouldn't have it in them, and then they see it happen, and they just can't go along."

In many ways, it's not so different than that clichéd thought experiment: if you had been a citizen of Germany during World War II, would you have stood up to the Nazis? Would you have hidden Jews? Allowed the yellow stars to go unchecked? We can speculate all we want, but until faced with the situation in real life—we just don't know what's really in us. Would we risk losing our tribe? Employment? Lives?

"I've argued that there's an epidemic of cowardice, and part of it is that we have too much regard for ourselves and too little experience of privation," says Weinstein. "People put their lives on the line for things that matter. Putting your job on the line for something that matters, that's very serious business, but it's not as serious as putting your life on the line."

In fact, when a nation is in jeopardy, like during times of war, it reserves the right to force you to put your life on the line. "When did we get the idea that we more or less have a right to be comfortable?" asks Weinstein. When we fail to speak up on things that matter, we abdicate our duty. "And those people who, when confronted by those forces, say the thing necessary to get the forces to stop, they are effectively pointing those forces at somebody else, right? When did we get the idea that we have the right to do that? In some sense, you are obligated to say 'no' when they level these accusations. You're obligated to do it because in saying no, their power is reduced, and the number of victims is reduced."

When people go along with things, hoping they'll just go away or go on to the next person, that's where that force gets its power. "I guess I'm becoming less patient with the many people who can't find it within themselves to stand up because, in effect, they are increasing the contagion of this dangerous coercive force," admits Weinstein.

Sometimes, throughout history, speaking up could be the most dangerous thing an ordinary human could do—and yet it is perhaps the most important thing, too. When too few people speak up for too long, dangerous ideas can take hold: McCarthyism, Nazism, Stalinism, Maoism, and more. All authoritarians have the same impulse: shut down speech they don't like. But it doesn't happen overnight. It's a matter of enough people going with it long enough, little by little. All it takes is for people to remain silent when those who dare speak out are silenced. First, they might lose their jobs for speech. Later, they are imprisoned for their speech. Soon enough, the price of speech rises to the ultimate cost: one's life. But it's not always easy to recognize that moment of no return when you're living in it. Are you overreacting or just seeing things clearly?

"We are in this moment," says Weinstein. "And I don't think we even know exactly what it's about, but I think that the fact that we can recognize the echo of history here tells us that this is very serious business, and it's not a moment at which you get to protect your comfort."

Many reject the idea that people are being silenced. They point to those who have been attacked for speaking against the new orthodoxy and have managed to become even more popular as a result. However, in making this argument, they fail to consider how silencing often happens in practice. How many people have been successfully silenced so that you never hear from them again? Or how many never even dared to speak in the first place in order to avoid the repercussions? Are they, quite possibly, the "silent majority"?

"Their point is that cancel culture doesn't exist because if it did, we wouldn't have heard of you. To the extent that anybody survives to talk about what happened to them, the phenomenon isn't real. It will only be real if it's so effective that nobody gets past it. I don't think you need to understand logic all that well to see the flaw there," explains Weinstein. "What's more, in a world of cancellation, is it any surprise that somebody who successfully fights back [can gain] popularity in the world . . . People are rooting for this. They're rooting for it because they fear it. They know they don't have the power to shut it down. And when they see somebody actually fight back and win, of course, that's popular."

He continues: "I'm not asking for anybody's pity, but it did happen. I mean, I was literally hunted down on my own campus. The police were literally told not to intervene. So it happened. And it can happen to you, too."

People may have become allergic to the idea of being on the right side of history, but Weinstein really does believe in it. "People will look back on this moment, and they will look at those who stood up," he says. "You don't want to be one of the people who made the wrong call."

But how do you know if you're on the right side? Look at who's on your side of the room. Are you happy with those standing next to you? "If the jerks [and the people you don't like or respect] all end up on the other side of the room and start cheering each on," you're probably on the right side. "If they are behaving like jerks, not speaking logically, and laughing at things that don't add up—you're doing the right thing."

Weinstein wants to be on the side of people who don't vilify others for holding different opinions or expressing them. "And I will also say there's something tremendously rewarding and fun about the kinds of people who are on [that] side of the room. It's very eclectic. Right? But isn't that delightful? That you don't have a bunch of carbon copies of some viewpoint and that you have a bunch of people from different sides of the political spectrum, very different backgrounds, very different approaches, who all agree, 'Hey, something's off, and I won't participate in it.'"

You don't want to be in the foxhole with anybody who can't be trusted, or, as he learned, who won't stand up for you, and, says Weinstein, we're headed for a foxhole.

Weinstein's battle didn't end at Evergreen. It was only preparing him for the next thing.

## Notes

On May 22, 2018, Weinstein provided testimony to the House of Representatives about the free speech crisis on U.S. college campuses. In his testimony, delivered to the members of the Committee on Oversight and Government Reform, he stated, "What is occurring on college campuses is about power and control," he said. "Speech is impeded as a last resort, used when people fail to self-censor in response to a threat of crippling stigma and the destruction of their capacity to earn." Notably, argues that this crisis will expand beyond college campuses in the years to come. See oversight.house.gov/hearing/challenges-to-the-freedom-of-speech-on-college-campuses-part-ii.

Vice has captured some of the Evergreen controversy, which resulted in protests. "Campus Argument Goes Viral As Evergreen State Is Caught In Racial Turmoil," YouTube, video uploaded by *VICE News* on June 16, 2017, www.youtube.com/watch?v=2cMYfxOFBBM.

Weinstein and Heying discussed their experiences at Evergreen on *The Ben Shapiro Show*. See "Bret Weinstein Revisits His Viral Encounter With

Student Protestors," YouTube, video uploaded by Ben Shapiro on September 28, 2021, www.youtube.com/watch?v=rQCqr86L-XI.

As part of Weinstein and Heying's $500,000 settlement with Evergreen, the school admitted no wrongdoing. Officials stated, "In making this agreement, the college admits no liability, and rejects the allegations made in the tort claim. The educational activities of Day of Absence/Day of Presence were not discriminatory. The college took reasonable and appropriate steps to engage with protesters during spring quarter, de-escalate conflict, and keep the campus safe." "Evergreen Professor at Center of Protests Resigns; College Will Pay $500,000," *Seattle Times*, September 16, 2017 (updated November 17, 2021), www.seattletimes.com/seattle-news/evergreen-professor-at-center-of-protests-resigns-college-will-pay-500000.

# 8 Don't Be Bullied into Silence

## The Lessons of Bret Weinstein (Part Two)

*A world in which reasonable people can disagree is one in which
there's actually something to discuss. The world we do live in
is where someone is inherently understood to be unreasonable
if they disagree—doesn't matter who they are. That is a toxic world.
That is a very dangerous world.*

*—Bret Weinstein*

What we know today may well change tomorrow.

Following events at Evergreen, Bret Weinstein launched the *Dark-Horse Podcast*, in which he and his wife, Heather Heying, discuss topics related to the so-called culture wars and the need for good science, governance, and civil discourse. As biologists, it was only natural that they would take a particular interest in COVID-19, including not just its origins and possible treatments but also the policies and protocols implemented to combat it. When Weinstein first began suggesting that the COVID-19 pandemic might be the result of a lab leak in China, he was accused of being a conspiracy theorist. At the time, the broad scientific consensus was that the virus originated in a bat—and any suggestion of a man-made origin was deemed not just wrong but also racist. Given the long history of past lab breaches and an overwhelming confluence of other factors, including the peculiar behavior of this virus, Weinstein believed the possibility of a lab leak was a legitimate worth exploring—no matter what the U.S. government and science journals at the time said. Weinstein and others who dared suggest it in those early days were stigmatized and called "wild-eyed conspiracy theorists," "grifters," and so on.

The trouble with being accused of being a conspiracy theorist, says Weinstein, is that you don't know if you'll ever be vindicated. Although today, the lab-leak hypothesis is taken seriously by the mainstream, vindication may never come, and that's a frightening prospect. "All you can do is try to be right."

The criticism Weinstein received when discussing the possibility of a lab leak didn't stop him from questioning other elements of the orthodoxy that came to surround COVID-19, including vaccine safety and efficacy and overall public health policy. Weinstein found the "ferocious pushback" he received for questioning what was being communicated and demanded by the authorities was "so aggressive, so incessant, and so personal" that it was "ten times as unpleasant as being accused of racism."

When the pandemic broke out, Weinstein, like so many others, watched the world turn toward the authoritarian. Discourse about public health policy was controlled, with governments often enlisting private companies to restrict any dissenting voice. The silencing of voices by big tech for what was dubbed as "misinformation" became commonplace. Even asking questions could result in deplatforming, demonetization, or other undesirable consequences. Those who were dependent on social media platforms for their livelihood often gave in and avoided certain topics. Some used coded language to get around the censors. "Absurd insanity," says Weinstein.

Weinstein gives the following example: After cosmologist Brian Keating had him and his wife on his podcast to discuss their new book—a completely nonpolitical book titled *A Hunter-Gatherer's Guide to the 21st Century: Evolution and the Challenges of Modern Life*—Keating discovered that the video he'd put up of the discussion was restricted on YouTube. Upon further investigation, Weinstein discovered that other videos in which he appeared were similarly restricted and would not show up in lists where they otherwise would.

It caused Weinstein to ponder: How did this phenomenon occur? Were there renegade people inside the tech companies who were manually interfering? Were there specific orders handed down from on high? More recent revelations have provided some answers. For example, after Elon Musk purchased Twitter and gave several journalists, including Bari Weiss and Matt Taibbi, access to the company's internal databases, the public learned through the Twitter Files that, at least within Twitter, certain accounts had indeed been "shadowbanned" or "deboosted" on a regular basis for alleged "misinformation," among other reasons. Further, a leaked email showed that the White House had made requests to deboost Facebook accounts spreading *correct* information as it related to the vaccine and the pandemic but which would increase vaccine hesitancy.

Was the same thing happening at YouTube? It certainly seems possible, if not likely. "The problem is that you really don't even know what role these forces play in your life," says Weinstein. "One of the most effective things they do is deny you information about where you even are. Are people listening to you in large numbers? Is your reach dwindling because you're saying things that people regard as false? You can't tell. And it's extremely disorienting."

For Weinstein, it's all rather frightening. After he and his wife were literally driven out of their professorships by a mob of "crazy people" for "saying the wrong things," they managed to rebuild a new career in the public eye. "That has a lot to do with our credibility," he says. "And now that is threatened with incredibly powerful forces that have the ability to alter who does or doesn't see our material and in what context they see it, what kinds of conversations it shows up in—and once again, our livelihood is threatened by people who do not appear to be honest brokers." Meanwhile, Weinstein is determined to continue to do what he believes to be the right thing and continue to share information that he believes to be correct—but what if, at some point, there remains no place for it to be shared because those wielding power reject his views and ideas?

The issue is not whether Weinstein is correct on all the points that he makes on his podcast or social media posts. He may very well be incorrect about some things, but the idea that some entity would have absolute authority on truth is a dangerous one. As we see throughout history, there have been plenty of times when governments and public institutions based policy on false beliefs—either because of error or intentional malice.

And yet, as Weinstein was being demonetized on YouTube, many people were actively cheering the company on. Meanwhile, the White House was dictating to tech companies what is misinformation and what is not. While the White House directing tech companies on the "truth" may have seemed innocent and well-intended enough to some, the legal implications of this are a bit murky. After all, tech companies technically did not have to comply and were not threatened with prison sentences or legal ramifications should they not do so—but when the White House (or a government agency) makes a request, it is naïve to believe that to deny it would not mean facing some sort of consequences, perhaps in the form of oppressive legislation, loss of political ad revenue, or some other form of interference. The White House, as the most powerful institution in the country, has countless levers at its disposal. Citing concerns around a potential breach of the First Amendment, in July 2023, a federal judge approved a preliminary injunction that will bar government officials from agencies such as the Centers for Disease Control and Prevention, Federal Bureau of Investigation, and the U.S. Department of Homeland Security from reaching out to social media companies with content moderation requests and concern.

Meanwhile, the general public—even if they've been lied to or been given the wrong information—tends to fall in line, especially when faced with some kind of existential or physical threat, whether real or perceived. "Because on some level people are . . . team players," explains Weinstein. In times of trouble, we as humans need someone to put our faith in something, whether it's our religion, our government, or our scientists. The alternative, the unknown, seems far too frightening.

Weinstein has taken a lot of heat for going against the grain, especially given his large and growing audience. He is often accused of "grifting," which he finds nonsensical because he is completely transparent about his views and opinions. He flatly rejects not only that claim but also the measurably worse one that says he's literally killing people with his "misinformation"—more specifically, that he is putting lives at risk by raising doubts about the effectiveness of vaccines and therefore contributing to vaccine hesitancy.

"I don't really even understand this critique because my sense is that the nonpartisan truth is that thousands, hundreds of thousands, maybe even millions of lives are at stake," explains Weinstein. "We all agree on that." So, he asks, "Isn't the right thing to do—to discuss what the actual facts imply, and what that suggests about how to minimize the harm of this pandemic? In other words, given what I believe to be true, and that we all agree that those lives are at stake . . . aren't I morally obligated to talk about my perspective? And people are absolutely free to ignore it, to challenge it, to describe what I've missed, to try to persuade me."

Weinstein says that one thing he shares with most of his critics is the desire to prevent harm and, from where he sits, keeping quiet may contribute to that unnecessary loss of life. "Lives depend on good policy. I have been absolutely steadfast about the danger that corruption poses to the functioning of society, and yes, that does mean lives are lost because our system is serving somebody else's objectives, not the public's."

In the most basic terms, that is how he understands the situation and is acting accordingly. He adds that he's got a long track record of being right in surprising places and that when he has been wrong, he has corrected what it is that he's gotten wrong—even if it may have been painful to do so. And, if he turns out to be wrong about anything he's been saying, he says that he'll make that known as quickly as possible. Besides, he asks, how do you even go about measuring the net impact— good or bad—of the information that he has shared? For example, he has advised his listeners to consume vitamin D, which is supported by studies to help protect individuals from COVID-19 and is generally considered to have few, if any, side effects when taken responsibly. If higher vitamin D levels across the population led to fewer transmissions, fewer hospitalizations, and fewer deaths, how would that not be a net good? As Weinstein maintains, he has always warned that COVID-19 must be taken seriously, that lives are at stake, and that people must adjust their behavior based on the best available evidence, which itself is subject to change over time.

"The best thing we can do is recognize that in some sense, we are all in on the idea that a full airing of all of the evidence, a vigorous defense of the positions by people who believe them, who present the evidence as carefully as they can ... that what comes out of that is a process that is likely to save more lives than it loses. To isolate my role and say you're killing people makes no sense, right? Because there's literally no way to find the people who will have been saved by what we're saying. And the idea that we are killing people is predicated on the idea that you're right about the evidence when one thing we should all agree on is that the evidence is quite confusing and requires careful analysis that isn't straightforward. The only reason people think it's straightforward is because there is a massive force shutting down those who point out the ambiguities."

To defend Weinstein's right to speak about COVID-19 doesn't mean having to agree with his opinions or findings. It is merely to support the idea that someone—especially someone with a scientific background and some level of understanding—has the right to present their ideas and to have those ideas be accepted, debated, or refuted. Weinstein may well be wrong, but he is allowed to be wrong, and it is up to the opposition to show he is wrong by proving its own case. He may also be right.

Indeed, Weinstein isn't arguing for people to accept what he says as the truth either. He only hopes that people who look at himself and his wife, people who have a background in a relevant discipline and who have looked very carefully into the evidence, arrived at a different conclusion than the one presented in the mainstream and have stuck to that conclusion despite being demonized for it and having their income opportunities limited because of it. He hopes that they can step back and realize that reasonable people can disagree on this topic and the interpretation of evidence.

"A world in which reasonable people can disagree is one in which there's actually something to discuss. The world we do live in is where someone is inherently understood to be unreasonable if they disagree— doesn't matter who they are. That is a toxic world. That is a very dangerous world. That is a world in which you can be led to do harm to yourself by officials who have been captured by some force that doesn't have your interests at heart."

When disagreement is not allowed, it also becomes incredibly difficult to know where each of us, or even a majority of us, stand on issues. This is especially true when those who managed to resist the intimidation against the odds have often been stigmatized, slandered, and had their livelihoods threatened. In the context of the pandemic, how widespread was our confidence in vaccines really? How about in our public health officials? Vaccine mandates? It's hard to know if only certain views are amplified, promoted, and rewarded while others are suppressed or punished. Weinstein calls this the "fog machine of war."

When even asking questions to better understand a position means that you risk being called a contrarian or a conspiracy theorist, people are effectively silenced. If you're accused of causing harm by merely casting doubt, many simply shut up.

"There is a sobering responsibility that comes with trying to dissect the evidence on these topics," admits Weinstein. "The reason that we were doing it in spite of that was that we believed it would do more good than harm [to speak up]." Weinstein argues that not speaking up allows people to escape taking personal responsibility. "The very act may cause people to lose their lives, but your fingerprints won't be on it if you haven't voiced an opinion that is outside of the mainstream. And so, it's very easy to point a finger at us and say, well, you've said things that are outside of the public health narrative, surely you're putting lives at risk ... But by pretending that the public health narrative is some sacred set of truths, you're also putting lives in jeopardy."

According to Weinstein, by staying silent and by telling people like him to do the same, people are not only abdicating their own responsibility but also trying to relieve others of responsibility. When people try to protect themselves and stifle debate, this leaves the "industrial strength narrative intact." "And frankly," he says, "I think this is a betrayal of the public." Weinstein points to the absence of vitamin D as a recommendation by public health officials as an example of such betrayal. "Are you really telling me that public health officials who've missed that one should be listened to on other topics without question?" Being silent, says Weinstein, is not a way to save lives: "Being silent is a way to not have your fingerprints on the deaths."

At the heart of this, says Weinstein, is a fundamental misunderstanding of how science works. "In their minds, they have this very childish notion of scientists being all in agreement ... and so they could speak as one. That's not how it works at all. And we're talking not only about science—we're talking about science in the context of complex adaptive systems, like people and pandemics and immunity. And what that means is that under the best of circumstances, when nobody has their thumb on the scale, things are still difficult to understand. And the way science progresses [is like this] ... people advance a perspective that explains a certain amount of the data and then maybe fails to explain some other amount. And then somebody else says, no, no, here is a simpler model that explains more and assumes less. And it actually does proceed through vigorous disagreement. That's what's supposed to happen."

Stigmatizing scientists with different views is not supposed to be part of that process. Today, the process is gamed. "It is unfortunately not the case that we can depend on science behind the scenes either in the public health institutions or in the university system to answer the question and tell us what they found because those systems are corrupted."

In evolutionary biology, explains Weinstein, there's a metaphor called the "adaptive landscape" in which opportunities are represented as peaks and obstacles to moving from one opportunity to the next are described as valleys. "We are definitely in an adaptive valley," he says. "We are watching chaos . . . in our technological environment, in our physiological environment, and those in charge of dictating our response are clearly at best incapable of providing useful guidance."

But, he says, it is necessary to go through an adaptive valley to get somewhere better. "So if our system is finally revealing itself to be less than up to the challenges of the twenty-first century, we can hope that that is the thing that will spur us to upgrade our system so that it can guide us." The trouble is that when you're in an adaptive valley, you don't necessarily know whether you are in transit to a better way of doing things or whether you are just headed further down into the abyss.

But Weinstein remains hopeful that this is the ugly process that is required in order for us to wake up and do better. Still, he says: "I fear that even if it is that moment, that we will not rise to the challenge."

Does this mean that we have to hit rock bottom to recover?

"You shouldn't have to hit bottom. One of the things Heather and I focus on . . . is the process by which humans bootstrap new software, and that doesn't require a crash. It requires consciousness and an awareness of where you are, and a commitment that we actually all have everything to gain in bootstrapping new and effective software when the old software has shown itself not to be capable of protecting and guiding us. So, there are circumstances in which hitting bottom is necessary. But those are usually things like addiction, right? Where something has to tell you that there's no future in what you're doing. And collectively, we're better than that. We can recognize that we are in trouble, and we can rise to the challenge."

Part of rising to that challenge is asking questions. There is no better way to keep the scientific process honest. At a time when it is commonplace to label certain ideas "misinformation," it is even more important to question whether an apparent "scientific consensus" was achieved organically or whether it was achieved because "they've intimidated everyone who would contradict it." When scientists aren't free to disagree without the aforementioned risks, how do we know that the consensus is real? If the scientific system has been breached, how do we know that we're not listening to, as Weinstein aptly puts it, "wolves in lab coats"?

## Notes

Weinstein has made multiple appearances on the *Joe Rogan Experience*, where he has discussed a number of topics, including COVID-19 and mRNA vaccines. See episodes #1494, June 18, 2020; #1671, June 22, 2021; #1705, September 9, 2021; and #1919, January 4, 2023, open. spotify.com/show/4rOoJ6Egrf8K2lrywzwOMk. He has discussed similar topics on *UnHerd with Freddie Sayers*. "Bret Weinstein: I Will be Vindicated over COVID," June 6, 2022, unherd.com/thepost/bret-weinstein-i-will-be.

For reporting on the Twitter Files, see Aimee Picchi, "Twitter Files: What They Are and Why They Matter," *CBS News*, December 14, 2022, www.cbsnews.com/news/twitter-files-matt-taibbi-bari-weiss-michael-shellenberger-elon-musk. For more on the pressure put on Facebook, see Ryan Tracy, "Facebook Bowed to White House Pressure, Removed Covid Posts," *Wall Street Journal*, July 28, 2023, www.wsj.com/articles/facebook-bowed-to-white-house-pressure-removed-covid-posts-2df436b7.

Weinstein is a prolific tweet proliferator on X at @BretWeinstein and hosts the Dark Horse podcast alongside his wife available on YouTube, Apple, and other platforms. You can also find him at bretweinstein.net.

# 9 Question the Narratives

## The Lessons of Aaron Kheriaty

*It's important to empower ordinary citizens to exercise their reasoning and logic because you don't have to be an expert in virology or public health to look and see that there are contradictions coming out of people's mouths and that they just logically don't hang together.*

*—Aaron Kheriaty*

Aaron Kheriaty was a professor of psychiatry and human behavior at the medical school and director of the medical ethics program at University of California–Irvine (UCI) Health but was eventually fired from that position on December 17, 2021, over his refusal to take the COVID-19 vaccine. This followed a lawsuit Kheriaty had launched earlier that year suing the University of California Board of Regents and Michael V. Drake, the system's president, stating that he should be exempt from the university's vaccine mandate because, as a practicing physician throughout the first year of the pandemic, he had already been exposed to this virus and thus had, as he claimed, "natural immunity." His stance was ultimately about personal choice. In that regard, he was anti-mandate rather than anti-vaccine per se.

His refusal to take the vaccine was based on his understanding of immunology, which was taught to him in medical school. What vaccines seek to do, he states, is to imitate infection-induced natural immunity. As a result, they sometimes come close to matching the protection provided by natural immunity, but they never meet or exceed the protection that natural immunity offers, with almost no exceptions to that rule. "I was all in favor of having a safe and effective vaccine come on the market for people that hadn't been infected with COVID," says Kheriaty, "especially for older individuals, who were the ones who were really at risk of bad outcomes from COVID."

This wasn't a conclusion Kheriaty reached lightly. He was actually part of the Orange County Vaccine Task Force, which meant that he had to consider many ethical questions, particularly in the early weeks of the vaccine rollout. Questions like: Who should be first in line? Should healthcare workers get priority? Essential workers? Kheriaty ultimately advocated for those most at risk. "I was never against the vaccines in principle for this virus, and the reports in the early data looked very good in terms of efficacy," he reiterates.

That said, he did have some concerns about safety because he was aware that clinical trials for the mRNA vaccines had been truncated. During the clinical trials, the participants who received the placebo and those who received the vaccines were followed on an ongoing basis and were evaluated frequently. Because the data gathering was consistent, if a participant in the trial got sick, the researchers had a chance to ascertain whether there was a link to the vaccine or not. But once the trial was ended early, under the claim that the vaccines were so effective that it would be unethical to not provide them to everyone, researchers had to rely on what's called "passive surveillance." This meant that safety data was collected through self-reports, which are cumbersome to collect, harder to interpret, and thus not ideal for finding causal links. That meant that we were now getting very poor, ongoing monitoring of safety, according to Kheriaty.

"One thing you have to understand is—whatever else you think of Big Pharma—vaccine manufacturers are very, very good at running clinical trials. I think it was not by accident that the clinical trial was stopped and the placebo arm was eliminated after three months. Because after the rollout, and based on research, especially from abroad, it became clear that after about four months, vaccine efficacy for the mRNA vaccines starts to decline. And by about seven or eight months, basically, in terms of infection, it's pretty close to the same as placebo. By about six months, it's below 50 percent effective, which is the threshold for FDA [Food and Drug Administration] approval. So, if they would have done a six-month trial, that vaccine probably would not have met that threshold for FDA approval. And they obviously would have had more time to look at adverse effects from the vaccines."

Further, Kheriaty points out that under U.S. law companies such as Pfizer are immune from liability for any vaccine they produce. "Several years ago, vaccine manufacturers convinced the federal government that it wasn't worth their investment to do research and development on vaccines unless they were protected from all liabilities from their products' harms," he explains. "I think that's an absurd argument. It's very clear how profitable these vaccines [have been]."

Although there have been voices of dissent among scientists and medical professionals—often labeled as "fringe voices"—many more have stayed silent. "Reason is, most of the researchers in medicine rely on pharma money for clinical trials for grants, or National Institutes of Health (NIH) money. And so, to kind of contradict the NIH-Fauci narrative is to risk being punished with not getting funded." Few scientists have been willing to take that risk, Kheriaty argues.

Kheriaty notes that it's important to understand that the various health services agencies are, as he puts it, "in bed with Big Pharma—It's very hard to distinguish them now." He cites the NIH co-owning the patent on the Moderna vaccine as an example. (The NIH gave Moderna $1.4 billion in funding toward the vaccine's development as well as lending its scientists and facilities.) The NIH ran the clinical trials on that vaccine, the FDA approved it, and the CDC made recommendations that became the basis for the mandates. "There's financial conflicts of interest left and right . . . All of these agencies are part of the Department of Health and Human Services. They all answer to the same cabinet-appointed secretary, and so there's money flowing from pharma back into Health and Human Services. And if you trace who the players are, it's like musical chairs; they just rotate from CDC to FDA to pharma."

There was a time, says Kheriaty, when there was a law prohibiting the direct-to-consumer advertising of pharmaceuticals. In the past, drugs could be advertised only to doctors via medical journals or conferences or salespeople. While there is a debate to be had whether greater consumer awareness of prescription drugs is good or bad, the reality is that nowadays, it's difficult to avoid being targeted by pharmaceutical ads, with ad spending rising annually. According to the Standard Media Index, the pharma industry spent $5.5 billion on ads for the first six months of 2022 alone. That potentially gives pharma companies a lot of influence over media organizations.

"It doesn't have to be overt," says Kheriaty. "It can be very, very subtle." He provides a hypothetical example wherein a TV show has him on as an expert, and the next week, the segment producer gets an email from Pfizer or a similar company suggesting that maybe they should reconsider having on someone like him: "We think you should have more credible sources on," the email might state. "Here's a list of people that know the vaccine data better than he does. No pressure. We just wanted to flag you on this. P.S. Our Vice President for Advertising Accounts will contact you next week regarding next year's ad buys." That kind of money, insists Kheriaty, can buy a lot of influence.

Unlike Kheriaty, plenty of scientists and medical practitioners were true believers, and they played a prominent role in the mainstream narrative that emerged. To the population at large, it thus appeared as if there was indeed a scientific consensus. But, says Kheriaty, "One thing you have to understand about scientists is that most scientists are extremely narrowly focused. They're studying one protein for ten years. They're obsessively focused on two or three molecules. They don't necessarily read outside of their narrow area of research. And they take [some things] literally on faith." He doesn't mean that as a criticism; this type of specialization is a necessity. It would be impossible for a single human to do all the research and read all the studies necessary to understand every specialized field: "We have to trust people we consider to be credible sources, and most scientists will just sort of go along with the mainstream narrative because that's the mainstream narrative." But what they tend to miss, perhaps naively, is that not everything that these conclusions are based on is credible. There are other factors involved, like financial and political interests—or other conflicts of interest we may not even be aware of.

As an ethicist, Kheriaty was predominantly concerned with the vaccine mandates: "I just thought that throwing the doctrine of informed consent because we're in a crisis or an emergency, and forcing a treatment on a competent adult—I thought that was a really bad idea." With other vaccines in the past, there were exemptions for medical and religious reasons, but in the case of the COVID-19 vaccines, there was no adequate leeway for those wanting to opt out. Meanwhile, what was at stake for people were their jobs and livelihoods, ability to go to school, scholarships, freedom of mobility, and more. He was against this type of coercion, which he found extreme. Further, whereas past vaccine mandates occurred only after a vaccine had been on the market for a number of years, this was all for a brand-new vaccine with no long-term data.

Prior to the vaccine rollout, physicians in California got a letter from the state's medical board stating that if they were to write any inappropriate mask exemptions or other COVID-related exemptions (which doctors understood to mean vaccine exemptions), their medical license could be investigated and they could be disciplined or lose their license altogether. This had a chilling effect on practitioners. "They never defined what constituted appropriate versus inappropriate. So, with that hanging over our heads, basically every physician in California [was] not writing exemptions. It [was] impossible to get a medical exemption in California because everyone [was] afraid to lose their license. I had a patient who went to her rheumatologist specialist about her autoimmune disorder, and this person told her: 'I don't think you should get the COVID vaccine because you're young and healthy and will be fine with COVID and I think this vaccine could worsen your autoimmune condition.' She said, 'Okay, can you write me a medical exemption?' Same physician said, 'No, I can't do that. Because I don't want to lose my license.'"

None of this sat well with Kheriaty. He published a piece in the *Wall Street Journal* arguing that university vaccine mandates were unethical, and afterward, a number of readers reached out to him to thank him. Some said that they had either medical or conscious-based reasons for not wanting to take the vaccination, yet they felt like they had no recourse. None of the people he heard from wanted to lie about their beliefs to get a religion-based exemption (where it was still a possibility).

"I thought, here's a person who's trying to be upright and honest and do the right thing, and they're getting steamrolled." When it came down to securing an exemption for himself, he thought, "Well, I could probably submit a religious exemption and they wouldn't ask me any questions about it because I'm the ethicist and I'm a physician, so I could take care of myself, but I wouldn't feel right about it." As a medical ethics professor, he just couldn't imagine himself getting up there and talking about moral courage and ethical integrity to students after that. "I just couldn't imagine myself doing that if I didn't put a stake in the ground on this one and stand up and try to stop the policy from going into effect."

When the university finally fired him, many of his students and colleagues reached out to him quietly. "There was a little bit of a silent conspiracy," he admits. "Between when I was put on leave and when I was fired, I think people felt like they couldn't talk about it at work." Then he reached out and wrote a letter to the faculty in residence and got some nice responses from that: "Many of them had reached out kind of privately and quietly, expressing support."

Kheriaty could have backed off and withdrawn his suit. "At one point, they were begging me to submit a religious exemption just to make my lawsuit go away." But he couldn't do it. "I don't know, maybe some of it is pride," he admits. "I'm not claiming that it's all virtue. Some of it is probably my personality. I've always been pretty comfortable being disagreeable. I've always sort of enjoyed challenging orthodoxies and conventional wisdom." There is a lot in medicine, he says, that may appear like common knowledge at first, but if you drill down on it and really dig deep, you realize that it doesn't actually have much evidence behind it. "It [starts] with kind of a shoddy paper in some journal," he says. Because of this phenomenon, he continues, "there's a lot of room in medicine for challenging what people think they know." He's also less bothered when people call him names. He used to make more of an effort to explain that he's not an antivaxxer, but he realized the name-calling still comes. "I really don't care what you call me . . . Either we can have a reasonable conversation, or [not]."

Kheriaty happens to have what he describes as a "healthy" mistrust of experts—even if many consider him to be one himself. He says that he's simply met too many of them that if you scratch beneath the surface, there's often not so much substance there. "They are not as smart as they think they are." He advocates that ordinary citizens become more aware of some of the big issues facing us in bioethics—because we all have a stake in it. Yes, having intellectual humility is important, as is understanding what it is that you might not know, but, he says, "It's important to empower ordinary citizens to exercise their reasoning and logic because you don't have to be an expert in virology or public health to look and see that there are contradictions coming out of people's mouths and that they just logically don't hang together."

A big part of what went wrong with the whole "trust the science" narrative is that so many people felt completely overwhelmed by the circumstances they found themselves in. "When the information is so complicated, and quite reasonably, most Americans don't feel equipped to sort through it, you have to be able to trust experts or other people or some institution or medicine as a whole—[a] kind of mainstream medical narrative. Because the alternative is that means you've got to sort through this and figure it out on your own. Most people can't process that. That's too much." But at the same time, the discourse around medicine and public health has been corrupted and suppressed.

"It has been so compromised that the possibility of meaningful debate was really quashed during the pandemic. If you ask questions, you're accused of killing people and so forth. I mean, it's just authoritarian and stupid. Most of our pandemic response has done more harm than good. It's been really destructive."

And for most people in the field, it has been incredibly difficult to push back. Kheriaty doesn't fault anyone for wanting to salvage their job. He thought about doing so himself, but he also knew he had the benefit of a medical degree. "It's not such a terrible thing to fall back on a private practice," he admits, "but most people don't have that—they are going to have to work for the healthcare system. It's going to be a very small minority that is going to be able to stand up and [push back]."

As someone who speaks publicly on issues of ethics and about pandemic policies, Kheriaty felt like he had to ask for an exemption, and he had the opportunity to make some noise around his request, too. But, he is quick to note, "Not everyone is going to be interviewed on TV when they get fired. Most people are just going to be forgotten, and when that happens, it's [not] going to change the policy. So I felt it was important to do it for those people. If these people are getting screwed over, I'll take their side on this."

Kheriaty has always had a sense that there is a link between an ethical life and a happy, flourishing life. "If people don't do the right thing, if they don't follow their conscience, usually things kind of fall apart." But if they do the right thing, he continues, "things sort of get better. I saw [ethics] as a way of trying to help make medicine better and help make things better, at least in the scope of the areas that I was working in."

Even long before the pandemic, Kheriaty had been fortunate enough to be exposed to thinkers and political theorists who had convinced him that democracies were not immune from totalitarian tendencies: "I don't have the prejudice that most Americans have, that those kinds of tendencies couldn't happen here or that we can behave any which way we want because we're kind of immune from that. I've never found that idea convincing. And so, when I see totalitarian tendencies, I try to name them."

He distrusts anyone who's not willing to debate openly and publicly, not willing to correct their position and say, "'You know, I said this last year, but I've kind of revised it based on new information, and now I think I was wrong.'" Put another way, anyone who doesn't embrace the scientific method—whether in the lab or in life.

## Notes

The opinion piece that Kheriaty co-authored with Gerard V. Bradley is worth a read to better understand his position. See "University Vaccine Mandates Violate Medical Ethics. College Students Aren't Guinea Pigs," *Wall Street Journal*, June 14, 2021, www.wsj.com/articles/university-vaccine-mandates-violate-medical-ethics-11623689220.

"A person may freely choose to accept medical risks for the benefit of others, as when one donates a kidney for transplant. But there is no moral duty to do so," Kheriaty told a reporter while speaking about his firing. Laura Newberry, "UC Irvine Fires Physician Who Refused to Get Vaccinated, Claiming 'Natural Immunity,'" *Los Angeles Times*, January 2, 2022, www.latimes.com/california/story/2022-01-02/uc-irvine-fires-physician-who-refused-to-get-vaccinated-claiming-natural-immunity.

Kheriaty's lawsuit against his school was ultimately rejected by the federal appeals court, which upheld his firing from UC Irvine. See Bob Egelko,

"Ninth Circuit Upholds Firing of UC Irvine Medical Ethics Director Who Refused COVID-19 Vaccine," *San Francisco Chronicle*, November 23, 2022, www.sfchronicle.com/politics/article/Ninth-Circuit-upholds-firing-of-UC-Irvine-medical-17607616.php.

For the lawsuit, see Kheriaty v. Regents of the Univ. of Cal. Casetext, November 23, 2022, casetext.com/case/kheriaty-v-regents-of-the-univ-of-cal.

On the natural immunity front, Kheriaty has been vindicated. A systematic review and meta-analysis in the *Lancet* on "the level and characteristics of protection from past SARS-CoV-2 infection against subsequent re-infection, symptomatic COVID-19 disease, and severe disease" concluded that natural immunity against severe disease and hospital admission has been strong and long-lasting for all variants to date (88 percent or greater at ten months post infection). COVID-19 Forecasting Team, "Past SARS-CoV-2 Infection Protection against Re-infection: A Systematic Review and Meta-Analysis," *Lancet* 401, no. 10379, P833-842 (March 11, 2023), www.thelancet.com/journals/lancet/article/PIIS0140-6736(22)02465-5/fulltext.

He remains a very active voice, speaking up for medical ethics and health policy. He writes a popular Substack (aaronkheriaty.substack.com), posts on X via @AaronKheriatyMD, and has most recently published a book about the rise of the biomedical security state, *The New Abnormal*.

He can also be found at aaronkheriaty.com.

# 10  Consider All Perspectives and Options

## The Lessons of Judith Curry

*[Y]ou make sensible policy decisions by hearing all perspectives and weighing all the options and alternatives and really understanding the uncertainties. Somehow, people have become allergic to this.*

*—Judith Curry*

Judith Curry is a climatologist who served as chair of the School of Earth and Atmospheric Sciences at the Georgia Institute of Technology prior to being pushed into early retirement. Tenure, as it turns out, is no obstacle to being pressured out of academia, particularly when you question human-caused climate change.

Curry's path from mainstream climate scientist to academic exile was a protracted one. It started in 2005 when she began engaging with blogs run by climate skeptics, in part because of critiques they had made about her own work. Her initial engagement with climate skeptics didn't generate much heat from her colleagues, however, and she simply found the interactions and challenges they offered interesting. But all of that changed when the "Climategate" scandal broke out in 2009. Hackers had stolen and leaked thousands of emails and documents from the University of East Anglia's Climatic Research Unit in Norwich several weeks before the Copenhagen Summit on climate change. Some claimed that these documents revealed that scientists had been manipulating climate data. Others countered that climate change deniers were misrepresenting the contents of the emails as part of a larger campaign to undermine climate change mitigation policy efforts.

This led Curry to become more vocal. She moved from commenting on blog posts to writing essays on her own blog on the integrity of climate science and how the scientific community needs to provide greater transparency with climate data, be respectful to critics and their work, and recognize how "tribalism" can negatively affect the peer review and assessment process. "Those were apple pie kinds of statements, but people got really upset," she recalls. "How dare I criticize the important people in the IPCC [Intergovernmental Panel on Climate Change]? Who was I anyways?"

The media soon took note. "I was standing up for what I thought was right, and I started to get more and more media attention." That included interviews with big media outlets like *Scientific American* and *Discover Magazine*, which were interested in the phenomenon of a mainstream scientist talking to skeptics. But media coverage suggesting that environmental science's findings and warnings about climate change might not be so certain was seen as a threat to many of her colleagues, who slowly began to ostracize Curry. "There were a few people in my department who were trying to take me down because I was chairman at the time, and they wanted me out."

What concerned Curry—even before she started writing about the problems in climate science—was both the politicization of science, which she saw everywhere, and the ways in which science was communicated to the public. She was particularly concerned with all the biases and consensus-building that a political lens brought to science and its communication. As a result, in her writing, she started exploring how psychological, philosophical, and social issues impacted science. This brought her to the attention of all sorts of people outside the climate field, such as lawyers, sociologists, and philosophers. She also started writing papers on the applied philosophy of science. "I thought that was a way forward for me academically, to get those papers published."

But as she relates, the questions she was raising and the attention she was generating eventually made it imperative for activists to take her down. "They called me every name in the book in op-eds [and elsewhere]."

She may have been Chair of the School of Earth and Atmospheric Sciences, but, as she puts it, "they knocked me off that pedestal." By then, the administration at Georgia Tech wanted her gone. They did not assign her to teach any classes or be on any committees. "I was completely marginalized. It was very clear: they didn't want me there." Instead of just sitting there and collecting her large salary, she decided to take her pension and quit. Curry now works in the private sector on projects that she finds interesting and has been working on a book about climate uncertainty and risk.

Of course, not everyone's in the same boat. Due to her age and work history, she was eligible to retire from the university with certain benefits. She's quick to note that if she had still been in her forties with a mortgage and college tuition to pay back, it would have been a different story. Now that she's a free agent, Curry doesn't have to worry anymore about how what she says is going to be perceived. "So I really have a lot of freedom that I didn't feel like I had at the university," she says. "People who are retired, people who are independent scientists, these are the people who don't have to worry about peer pressure or administrative pressure or getting grants or whatever. I mean, you have to tow the party line if you're going to succeed in that system, but it's the independent and the retired people who are the freest. So it's a luxury in a way."

She says she's been marginalized not for what she says scientifically but rather for how her words and writing are perceived: "People like me aren't all that far from the mainstream of scientific thought. But it's the fact that we criticize the process and that we criticize certain things—

including the behavior of certain people and the public statements of certain people—that gets us ostracized. Where we sit scientifically is well within the envelope. But it's really more the social aspects of daring to criticize."

Criticism, after all, is inconvenient. It gets in the way of people's reputations and seats at important tables. It gets in the way of awards and grants from foundations. "They have this whole little empire built up on this stuff. So it's not about science anymore; it's about their whole persona, and they are out to defend that. I mean, some of it is politically driven, but most of it is really just more professional ego and protection of their status." In other words, for many scientists, criticism threatens their self-image or even sense of self-importance.

The truth is that for a long time, Curry didn't really pay all that much attention to the IPCC. In fact, she felt that supporting it was the responsible thing to do until she herself got caught up in the politics and lack of nuance that seemed to surround all discussions about climate. When she coauthored a paper in *Science* that warned of the likelihood of hurricanes becoming more intense as a result of climate change, for example, the media was quick to sensationalize the work, but she knew that there were more unknowns than the media headlines suggested and that more vigorous debate and investigation was needed. She could see how this type of sensationalized coverage not only affected public sentiment but also might influence the work and words of other scientists. Then, during "Climategate," when she read the leaked emails, she could no longer ignore the bullying and pressure to conform to an overarching narrative and decided she had to step outside her own silo to fully understand the issue.

"The challenge for any individual scientist is that they have just a few narrow paths that they research on," she explains, "and so it's natural for a much broader body just to accept the established consensus. So, at that point, I had to do an about-face and say, 'Well, I'm going to play this different kind of a role. I need to become more of a generalist.

I need to understand all (or most) aspects of this and become conversant in policymaking, energy, economics, and so on." That is why her blog became a focus for such a range of topics, a change that gave her a much more useful perspective in the climate change debate. Prior to that, because she was only working in a couple of areas, it was natural for her to accept the general conclusion in all the other areas that she wasn't working on.

"Any scientific topic that gets politicized, anything where there's money and power, there's a lot at stake on both sides," says Curry. She cites GMO (genetically modified organism) discourse as another example. "People were getting canceled left and right," she says. The hard boundaries placed around any discussion of COVID, including its origins, have been another highly salient illustration. When things get politicized to the extent that they have, she says, people stop trusting the government, science, and experts. "The more they try to enforce things, the bigger the backlash, and you get this big spiral, and it gets out of control."

Even when it's not a politicized field, it's very hard for contrary ideas to get any headway, she says. "In science and academia, you often get this kind of ostracism and gatekeeping. It's professional ego, and people want to control the dialogue, they want to control the money, they want to control who gets the awards, and on and on it goes. So it's just what happens."

In the private sector, she says, if something really doesn't make sense or someone is terrible at their job, they are not going to make it for long because they have financial accountability to the company. It won't keep them there for long if they are not contributing to a positive outcome. But in academia, it's different. "These kinds of people get tenure and get sheltered. And some of these slightly pathological personalities end up accruing power in professional societies and as editors of journals. So they're protected in academia, these slightly pathological personalities, whereas it's much harder for them to survive in the private sector. Academia is a peculiar protected culture that allows that kind of stuff to thrive."

The problem is that culture discourages the kinds of disagreements that are necessary for the advancement of our understanding of science. Differences will never be understood or acknowledged unless people speak up, says Curry. "We need to hear the difference. We need to understand the differences. We need to see if there's anything we can resolve . . . We have to acknowledge the difference. We have to make our decisions in a way that doesn't necessarily pick the winner or the losers, but that accommodates viewpoints in some sort of a rational way." There's a lot of uncertainty in just about everything, and there can be genuine disagreements in the most quantitative fields, even in mathematics. "When it comes to anything that relates to complex societal issues, there's not much that's simple and completely understood." Disagreement, says Curry, moves the whole field of climate science forward and gives scientists new ideas to explore. "It's also how you make sensible policy decisions by hearing all perspectives and weighing all the options and alternatives and really understanding the uncertainties. Somehow, people have become allergic to this."

She says that scientists as a whole today aren't speaking truth to power; rather, they have become more about "speaking consensus to power." If you can declare consensus or get yourself within the in-group, then you have power and can call the shots. But ultimately, that means that you end up "sending science down a rat hole [and] making lousy decisions. So where does that leave you?"

Meanwhile, there's no one really scrutinizing these claims of consensus. Instead, they are being reflexively and uncritically promoted. "Journalism has changed a lot," explains Curry. "They used to really be the ones to critically evaluate stuff, and now they're all tribal. They all sound alike."

In the Wikipedia entry about Curry, she's described as a contrarian scientist and as part of the climate change denial blogosphere. Are these accurate assertions by the website's volunteer editor brigade? "There's massive warfare over my Wikipedia page," responds Curry. "There's a few hardcore people defending me and there's people trying to [take me down]. I'm just astonished. It's kind of crazy."

Curry's blog has been simultaneously described as both the most objective and intelligent climate blog on the internet and as a climate denial blog. Curry sees herself as a critic of the way that public climate science is done and the way that the public debate has evolved. She sees herself as a critic of the IPCC and of people prematurely declaring consensus. She doesn't even see herself as a contrarian. "I'm not that far out of the side of the envelope," she reiterates. "It's well within the likely range even. But I am a critic, and because I have criticized the behavior of some scientists and I have criticized the IPCC, this is why I have been ostracized . . . I should be regarded as a critic. But not a contrarian, a critic."

Does this mean that Curry does indeed believe that climate change is caused by humans? What puts one inside the envelope versus slightly outside of it? "You have to say that climate change is 100 percent man-made," she responds. "If you don't say it's 100 percent man-made, then you're a denier. Of course, it's not 100 percent."

What's really behind this absolutist thinking? Is it the idea that if it's 100 percent man-made, it means that humans can do something about it? Is it about our ability to control?

"Yeah, it's right. And in all honesty, it's a little bit more of Democratic political thinking [of] 'we can manage things,' whereas Republicans just say, 'Let it go and let whatever happens, happen.' So it's a Democrat thing. Their mindset is more of a technocratic 'we can control this.' [But we] can't control it. Whenever the genie's out of the bottle, you can't put it back in. Thinking you're going to reverse this . . . even if it is all caused by CO2, you're not going to reverse it on any kind of meaningful timescale."

If we accepted that perhaps it is not within our powers to control the atmosphere, as she argues, we might be better served by shifting toward investing into coping with these changes. "Exactly. That's adaptation, trying to increase our resilience. To me, that's a sensible strategy. And then slowly figure out what a twenty-first-century energy infrastructure should look like. Solar probably makes sense because it's not a big infrastructure investment. But wind farms are massive infrastructure and huge land use footprint. [With a lot of current solutions] you just exchange one set of problems for another set of problems. There's a lot of technologies under development that will eventually work if we wait five or ten years."

As someone who ended up pushing against the orthodoxy and received sufficient pushback that she felt she had no choice but to resign from Georgia Tech, Curry is conflicted about giving advice to anyone else considering doing the same. "If you really speak up and investigate," she says, "your career will be stunted." She didn't even know what to tell students who wanted her name on their paper. "With a certain slant of paper, we'll get it published in *Nature*, and it will help them succeed in their career, but I can't put my name to that." That's one of the other reasons she quit; she didn't know what to say to students. And she couldn't ask them to be bold either. "I started risking [my career] when I was in my late fifties," she notes. If she was younger and had dependents who relied on her financially, she would have been in a different position. Maybe she never would have spoken up.

Courage is tougher when you've got college tuition to pay off, a mortgage, and your whole career ahead of you to jeopardize, she reiterates. "It's very chilling. It promotes conformity. And that's not what university should be about, so it's a sad state of affairs."

Few people, says Curry, have the luxury to be free to say what they wish. Social media has made speaking up particularly dangerous for academics, but it's become a necessary tool to get attention for your work and "move up the food chain." Still, she warns, "It doesn't take much for the herd to turn on you."

## Notes

For those interested in opinions on climate outside of what is perceived as consensus, you might find Curry's op-ed on the topic worth reading. In it, she suggests that the climate is "less sensitive to increases in carbon-dioxide emissions" than is often assumed by policymakers: "The Global Warming Statistical Meltdown," *Wall Street Journal*, October 9, 2014, www.wsj.com/articles/judith-curry-the-global-warming-statistical-meltdown-1412901060.

She has also been a guest on Jordan Peterson's show to discuss climate change, prediction models, and why dissent is important in science. Jordan B. Peterson Podcast, ep. 329, "The Models Are OK, the Predictions Are Wrong," February 6, 2023, available at www.youtube.com/watch?v=9Q2YHGIIUDk.

*Nature* has an extensive interview with Curry where she shares her criticism of the Intergovernmental Panel on Climate Change (IPCC) and argues that its in need of reform. She also criticizes the scientific community's increased hostility toward those who dissent. It's an excellent overview of her story. Michael Lemonick, "Climate Heretic: Judith Curry Turns on Her Colleagues," *Nature*, November 1, 2010, www.nature.com/articles/news.2010.577.

She also writes about climate on her website judithcurry.com and on X @curryja.

# 11 Go on the Attack

## The Lessons of Cliff Mass

*Every time I've gone on the attack, it's worked out very well.*
*So, going in on the attack is key here.*

—*Cliff Mass*

It would be accurate to describe meteorologist Cliff Mass as rather outspoken. He's a fully tenured professor of Atmospheric Science at the University of Washington who, at a senior stage of his career, has his own popular blog and a podcast. He specializes in weather prediction and modeling, with a research emphasis on weather features of the western United States. Over the years, he's become known as an outspoken critic of some climate science orthodoxies, such as claims that climate change plays a critical role in extreme weather events and that the earth is facing an existential threat of extinction due to humankind's role in climate change. Although he does acknowledge that emissions caused by greenhouse gases from burning fossil fuel and other human sources contribute to climate change, his views have made him controversial in some circles. Still, this did not stop him from having a segment on KNKX public radio, Tacoma's National Public Radio affiliate, titled *Weather with Cliff Mass*.

He has always been pretty frank, even when he was younger—though in the past, he was a bit more careful than he is today about sharing his views. "I can take chances," he admits. "I like to look from the outside and point out issues, but I'm not *so* brave, because my position is secure." While his career might be relatively safe, at least from his point of view, there are certainly social consequences to being so outspoken. He admits that, indeed, a number of people have tried to make his life miserable, but he says he's since become accustomed to this: "One discipline I had to learn is not to get myself deeply hurt by people saying or doing things. That is a training that one needs to gain when you're in this kind of space."

So, how does one develop such a pertinent skill, exactly? "It's just telling yourself that if you're out there saying things that are not popular, there is a group of people that are going to try to hurt you and try to silence you. And the fact they're trying to do that means you're succeeding. It's a measure of success." To paraphrase Victor Hugo, if you don't have any enemies, then you haven't stood up for anything important in your life. "We are in an extremely scary time now," says Mass, "where a large group of people are trying to suppress the diversity of viewpoints, and I think democracy depends on [being able to express them]."

According to Mass, the people who have chosen to speak up and fight for the ability of others to do so without fear of losing their jobs or facing mobs eager to go after them are doing important, meaningful work, but he wonders how those who sit around and keep their mouth shut will look back on their silence when they're in their eighties or nineties. He says that many people, including colleagues, agree with his views or have other views that run counter to the mainstream but are afraid to speak up. "I get a lot of people who tell me they are afraid," he says. He understands. "But I also tell them that we need enough people to come stand up against this stuff. Just like in Germany, a lot of people kept silent, and bad things happened. And in the fifties, a lot of people got their careers destroyed [during McCarthyism]. [Then there] was the rush to go to war in Iraq . . . One time after the other, a lot of people kept silent, and very bad things happened."

A big lesson he has learned is that when you stick up for yourself, often those going after you back off. "A lot of these people are bullies," he says, "and when you stick up to a bully, they back off." The key is not to be passive—you can't just take the abuse. Go on the attack, go after them. They won't like it. "Every time I've gone on the attack, it's worked out very well. So, going in on the attack is key here." This might be a difficult pill to swallow for a nonconfrontational person, but Mass is clear on this point: "I hate to tell you, but you need an offense. That's the way it works. You just can't fight a successful war with just defense."

Part of his motivation to not only speak out but also fight for the right to do so is rooted in the belief in the concept of *tikkun olam*, a Hebrew phrase that translates as "repairing the world." The Jewish community takes the idea as a call to action to help make the world a better place through kind acts, charity, and improvements. "I kind of like fixing things, you know?" he says. "I see something that I'm convinced is wrong or problematic, and I'm kind of driven to try to fix it."

Nowadays, as far as freedom of speech goes, things are seriously broken, he argues. "It's very serious," he emphasizes. "It's very scary. I've lived through a time where I remember a different environment, so it's very jarring to see what's happened." Those who have lived under authoritarian and totalitarian systems understand the danger and warning signs far better than most, he says, such as those who emigrated to the West from China and witnessed the Chinese Cultural Revolution or those who came from the Soviet Union and understood oppressive censorship. Today, they are among the strongest voices opposing what's been happening to speech freedoms in recent years. "They've seen this story—they know where it goes."

Although Mass has been critical about the climate change discourse—particularly the hype and exaggeration there—he's proven to be a difficult target for his opposition because of his authority on the subject. "They can't shoot me down technically," he says, "so it's a particularly good place for me to play around." But this hasn't stopped his opponents from finding other ways to attack him, such as when he writes on subjects unrelated to his scientific expertise. For example, he became a bigger target when he made a post on his blog comparing the riots associated with the George Floyd protests in Seattle in July 2020 to Kristallnacht, when Jewish businesses, homes, and synagogues were looted and violently destroyed across Nazi Germany in November 1938. His blog post read: "Seattle has had it[s] Kristallnacht, and the photos of what occurred during the past weeks are eerily similar to those of 80 years ago." Although Mass saw a likeness between the two events, many found the comments offensive and inaccurate. Under pressure, KNKX issued a statement announcing it would immediately stop airing his weather segment, stating that Mass drew "distorted, offensive parallels between protesters and Nazi Brownshirts. We abhor the comparison and find it sensationalized and misleading—it does not reflect who we are and what we stand for at KNKX."

"I didn't say it was the same thing," explains Mass. He had read a lot about the events leading up to the Holocaust and felt that what he had been seeing on the streets of the United States was very reminiscent. What was missed in the outrage over his post was that many Jewish businesses were actually the ones being attacked in Seattle. "They were targeting Jewish businesses," explains Mass, a critical context to include. But in his mind, the blog post was just the pretext the station needed to get rid of him. "The radio station was ready to get rid of me before then because of my climate stuff, so they were just using it as an excuse."

This raises the question, if someone has a show on a radio station but says something that the station disagrees with, how should a station handle this objectionable speech? For Mass, it depends in part on where and when the "objectionable" speech occurred. Referring to his own case, he says, "If I didn't say it on the radio station or the TV station? If it was my own private speech, I don't think they should touch it as long as it's not illegal. Public radio stations should respect freedom of speech more than anyone, frankly."

Mass also points out the irony of a public radio station saying his comparison of violent protestors with Nazi Brownshirts was offensive. As he notes, many news outlets and commentators regularly made comparisons between the Trump administration and Nazi Germany, often directly calling Republicans or anyone left of center Nazis. "So it was fine for them to use that Nazi imagery for other people."

The proliferation of news outlets that worry more about catering to their audience than about reporting facts has caused much of the destruction of bipartisanship. According to Mass, the rise of social media has only made the situation worse. "It's been a very, very strong stimulator of this," he says. "It's allowed people to simply go into their silos in a very negative way. And certain political parties have actually tried to take advantage of it to try to become overly partisan." While part of the increased bias can be attributed to the need to generate more clicks, economics have also played a significant role in the decline of media as it transformed to a predominantly web-based format. Mass recalls science journalists spending days on a story and verifying information before it went to press. "That doesn't happen anymore." The decline of the U.S. education system has also had a profound role in this growing polarization. Newer generations do not understand the vital role discussion, debate, and dialogue play in solving problems and maintaining a healthy society. "Young students do not take civics classes very much anymore. The ignorance about history is unbelievable."

Mass cites his own treatment as a case in point. Rather than engage him in debate, his critics tolerate no discussion or dialogue. Their one and only response is to aggressively try to shut him down and shut him up. Why not just let the facts speak for themselves and prove him wrong, he asks, if he is, indeed, wrong? According to Mass, these elevated temperaments and sense of righteousness speak to something else.

"[Climate change] has become a religion," responds Mass. "This is a religion now, and I'm the worst possible person. I'm an apostate priest. No one is hated more than an apostate priest. And since they can't get to me technically, all they can do is call me names. I mean, I've spent my lifetime learning about the weather and climate of this region. I have extremely good credentials, and they know that, so they can't get me on the technical stuff. They can't get me on my background. I'm a very frustrating issue for them." He points out that he's never heard anyone demand that others believe in gravity or radiation, two things that are obviously real, but for some reason, the same cannot be said about climate change. Any kind of disbelief—even in the form of a genuine question—is not allowed.

Just like many other religions, the faith of climate change happens to have an apocalyptic side to it. "The end of the world story, right?" he points out. "And particularly, if you don't do what they say to do, there's going to be the end of the world." As classic religions have weakened, climate has filled some of that void. In a way, it's not even so far from the sun god or the weather gods of yesteryear, says Mass. People are always searching for meaning in life, and everyone has different ways of finding it. The religion of climate change is just one more avenue in that pursuit.

And like apostates from traditional religions, Mass has paid a price for expressing his views—such as losing friends. If he could do things over again, he says he might choose to word some things a little differently, but otherwise, he does not regret the path he's chosen. "I mean, it's definitely affected me, but the backlash goes both ways. It's not all negative." As a result of his willingness to speak truthfully about what he believes, he has managed to reach and connect with a lot of people who appreciate what he has to say. He also gets to speak with people he wouldn't have otherwise connected with. This is reflected in the success of his blog and podcast, which are both doing well in terms of audience reach and finances. "I still have that, and I'm not losing [it]. So it's not all negative."

At the same time, the campaign to get him kicked out of his university is ongoing. But Mass, true to his words, has been quick to go on the offensive when needed. When threatened by university administrators, for example, he has been able to mobilize his blog's readers for support. In one instance, for example, the university put out a press release stating that his position was in no way threatened after receiving thousands of emails from his readers.

This type of support is very welcome for Mass, in large part because of the lack of public support he receives from his colleagues. Mass really wishes that they would speak out more publicly and for a freer exchange of information, but at the same time, he understands when they say, "Listen, I agree with you. You've got a lot of it right, but I don't want to make any waves. I'm worried about my getting my grants or whatever it is. I want or need to advance to associate professor or full professor." It's something for each person to decide for themselves. "It would be good if they did it, but I'm not going to tell people to make a life-changing decision that could potentially, you know, change their life."

At the same time, Mass worries that we risk losing our civilization if we don't fight for the ability to talk things out. "You can't have a functioning democracy without it," he insists. "Civilization is a thin veneer, and people don't realize how thin it is." When it comes to climate change, he says, you can't deal with it unless you're dealing with the facts first. And you can't do that without allowing scientists to talk openly and freely.

## Notes

To learn more about Mass's views on the weather and climate, a good jumping-off point is his interview with *Northwest Now* on PBS, April 15, 2021, www.pbs.org/video/cliff-mass-hac01h.

For coverage of Mass's views toward climate, see Hal Bernton, "Seattle Meteorologist Cliff Mass Sparks Controversy by Diving into Heat Wave Climate Science," *Seattle Times*, August 3, 2021, www.seattletimes.com/

seattle-news/seattle-meteorologist-cliff-mass-sparks-controversy-by-di-ving-into-heat-wave-climate-science.

For coverage of his "brownshirts" comment and subsequent removal from the air, see Christine Clarridge, "KNKX Takes Meteorologist Cliff Mass off the Air after He Likens Seattle Protest Actions to 1938 Nazi Pogrom," *Seattle Times*, August 7, 2020, www.seattletimes.com/seattle-news/knkx-takes-meteorologist-cliff-mass-off-the-air-after-he-likens-seattle-protest-ers-to-germanys-brownshirts-on-infamous-kristallnacht.

Mass blogs at cliffmass.blogspot.com, hosts a podcast called *Weather with Cliff Mass* on Apple, and is on X at @CliffMass.

# 12  Know Which Hill to Die On

## The Lessons of Winston Marshall

*People who say that cancel culture doesn't exist, what they don't
realize is when artists like JK Rowling [is targeted] who can
weather those storms . . . it's the younger artists and the less
successful artists who are self-censoring. And that's
[the aspect of] the culture that's so dangerous.*

*—Winston Marshall*

Until recently, Winston Marshall was best known as the banjoist, lead
guitarist, and sometime songwriter of the popular Grammy Award–winning British folk rock band *Mumford & Sons*. In March 2021, however,
he found himself making headlines for decidedly less musically oriented
reasons when his career—and life—went into a bit of a spiral due to a
single tweet in which he praised a book called *Unmasked: Inside Antifa's
Radical Plan to Destroy Democracy*, written by American journalist Andy
Ngo. The tweet read, "Congratulations @MrAndyNgo. Finally had to
time read your important book. You're a brave man." Outrage quickly
followed. with some charging that he "endorsed fascism." Marshall initially apologized for his praise and said he'd take a break from the band
"to examine blindspots," but he later changed his mind and wrote an

article that defended his support of Ngo, expressed regret for his initial apology, and announced his decision to permanently leave *Mumford & Sons*. He said he didn't want his bandmates to be affected by anything else he might say. "I could remain and continue to self-censor," he wrote, "but it will erode my sense of integrity. Gnaw my conscience. I've already felt that beginning."

During the pandemic and lockdowns, Marshall spent his time tweeting about books he liked and putting up Instagram photos. He didn't even have many followers on Twitter at the time—perhaps just 3,000 or so. He happened to come across Ngo's book and found it interesting. "Antifa is really not reported on much in a lot of mainstream media, and so I felt compelled to tweet about that." Marshall felt Ngo was brave in exposing far-left extremism and that his work and voice were largely ignored by left-wing mainstream media. Beyond that, there was nothing extraordinary or controversial about the tweet. Indeed, he had been tweeting about a range of books—including Mao's Little Red Book. "I certainly wouldn't approve of Mao's Little Red Book, but I read that at a similar time," he says, "and I remember tweeting about a brilliant book by James Bloodworth about Amazon working conditions, so I thought this was just another book worth recommending and it had just been published."

The next thing he knew, the whole thing exploded into what Marshall refers to as "one of those Twitter storms in a teacup." His seemingly insignificant tweet was being covered by *The View* and Tucker Carlson. "I'm like: How did this f-cking happen?" And as much as people like to say that Twitter isn't real life, his tweet quickly began to affect his real life, including his relationships with friends and his professional work. "A radio station threatened to drop us, or maybe dropped us," he recalls. "One festival I was due to DJ at canceled me from the lineup because the headliner they had hoped to book condemned me on Twitter. So I was literally finding actual professional repercussions for reading a book."

It was an emotional weekend.

Marshall issued an apology shortly after. "At that time, I was totally open to the idea that maybe there was something I didn't know. Because when you're criticized, a normal human being listens and goes, well, what do I not know? So I should apologize because it seemed like I'd upset a lot of people and, obviously, the repercussions from my opinion were affecting my bandmates. So I made the apology."

Would he have made the apology if the impact was on him alone? If bandmates were not involved? "It's hard to play that counternarrative," admits Marshall. "But I think if I was a lone actor, things would have panned out very differently. But when you're in a band, you have accountability to each other. And not only that, I would say that I love them very much, and I didn't want them to face the repercussions or the negativity that I was facing. I didn't think it's fair on them that they should be brought under the bus with me."

At that point, Marshall was also particularly open to being wrong. He spent a lot of time digging into the subject and looking into all the negative things he was being told about the author. "I didn't see actual evidence for it," he says. Meanwhile, he says, far-left extremist activists had tinkered with his own Wikipedia page to say that he was a fascist. This was "ludicrous beyond belief, not least because I'm the progeny of Holocaust survivors," he says, annoyed at even having to say that. ("But it just adds kind of a better color to how ridiculous the situation is.") It also allowed him to experience first-hand the types of things they were doing to Andy Ngo. "It actually just made me think, 'Oh, I was right. He really was a brave guy that has to put up with this shit on a daily basis.'"

Sometime after Marshall's apology letter came out, he learned that Ngo had been physically attacked by far-left extremists in Portland. It played on his conscience. "I was literally not sleeping," he recalls, "because I felt like I had sort of supported the lie that he was he was in any way a bad guy."

Marshall was facing a horrible conundrum. He knew if he were to openly say what he really thought, his bandmates would suffer for that, and it wouldn't be fair to them. Yet, he felt a duty to speak. "After much, much deliberation, thought, and prayer, I felt that the only way I could deal with this situation was to leave the band." He lost a lot by leaving, but he felt a sort of relief, too. "The effect it had on my soul, my integrity, and on my conscience was really a profound thing that I haven't been able to articulate quite yet. But I might be able to do it one day. I hope I might be able to," he says.

When Marshall reversed course and wrote a piece on *Medium* (later reprinted by *Newsweek*) in which he defended Ngo, separated himself from Mumford & Sons, and vowed to practice his newly found public speech, he got many positive messages from various artists. Most of the messages, however, were not shared on social media. They were shared privately. "I guess it's probably difficult for a lot of them," he says. "It's difficult for people to talk out on certain issues, and so there was a lot more private stuff than public stuff, which is fine . . . Who would want the hell that happened to me? Anyone would want to avoid that. So I can see why they wouldn't go public necessarily with showing their solidarity." But, he says, he also got a lot of public support from people he respects.

That solidarity aside, having a supportive, close-knit family was especially valuable to him. "It's been the great privilege of my life actually having two parents that love me deeply and care for me . . . I felt that gave me much [support] in that difficult, difficult time."

After he wrote his piece for *The Spectator*, he says that he received an unbelievable amount of positive private messages from all sorts of people—from just about every profession imaginable. "And when I say thousands, I mean that literally—that's not an exaggeration. It was very moving." But what he found to be concerning is that many of these messages came from professionals who can't afford to be sacked. "I'll be alright. I'm a big boy. I've got savings. The band's done very well. I'm going to be fine. I can rebuild. But there are people who have careers where they built those careers up for decades. That's not something easy to give up. They have families, they have wives, they have children, they have husbands who depend on them and their salary. And so that's what's worrying. The people who are in that place where they can't [afford to speak up] because they can't afford to lose everything. That's something that our culture is suffering from at the moment."

Based on the messages he received and continues to receive, Marshall sees clearly this is a phenomenon affecting society at large, not just journalism or the arts. "There are various topics where people fear losing everything if they speak out on them, which is really not a healthy place for us to be in." This silencing culture is "a really serious problem," says Winston, "because if people can't talk about this stuff, that means that the ideas that they cannot talk about are not challenged. And if they're not challenged, then they're open to turning into pretty bad ideas. And so, if you want to actually get rid of these extremist or bad opinions, you need to engage with the people." When you stop engaging with bad ideas, they grow more extreme and create worse outcomes for society. "That's why you see the growth of these huge conspiracy theory sites because people aren't even engaging on the bit where those people are occasionally right."

Marshall acknowledges he lost some friends during this process, but on the plus side, his openness has paved the way for new relationships with like-minded individuals. "You get a lot of people reaching out who feel the frustration and feel like they're in similar positions in their professions and in their worlds and communities. And that's kind of a wonderful thing. I've made wonderful friends actually as a consequence of it. I guess once your head is above the parapet, people do reach out to you, and that's kind of very encouraging and lovely." As for the relationships he's lost, he says, "Maybe I'll be reunited with my old friends too one day."

When you're a person in the public domain, you need to be prepared for the incoming storm. Although, these days, thanks to social media, anyone can become a mass target. Still, advises Marshall, it's probably wise to think carefully about the issues that one is going to speak out on and be prepared. "The mistake I probably made was that I didn't quite realize that I was stepping on a mine with that one and so didn't get to choose the hill [I] die on."

But, he says, there are some people who have probably spent more time reflecting on which hill it is that they are prepared to die on and understand what it is that comes with being outspoken about certain subjects.

Winston's advice to anyone considering freeing their own voice is to think about it carefully: "Don't just do it by accident. Be strategic about it, instead of it happening to you, and it's out of your control."

In the aftermath of everything that has happened, Winston feels freer than ever. When Mumford & Sons released its first three albums, they were never really asked about politics. But when they released their fourth album in 2018, something noticeable had changed. At its release, they were never asked about music. "That was sort of the difference in the culture," says Marshall. But, of course, this change signaled not a climate where free expression is valued but rather one in which conformity is. For example, when a photo of Marshall and psychologist Jordan Peterson surfaced around that time, Marshall understood he couldn't speak honestly about it. "I knew there'd be backlash, and I didn't want the people around me to suffer because of that." He had the same sentiment when he participated in all-important press junkets, which were set up to promote the band. In this newer climate, you'll get provocative political questions that merit fifteen-minute answers, but the interview itself is limited only to five minutes, and all you have time for is a one-liner. "How could you possibly answer these questions with one line?" So, as an artist, the choice is either shake your head and go along with whatever is being said to avoid conflict or respond as best you can in a pithy way and accept whatever negative press that comes your way as a result of the soundbite. For many artists, following the path of least resistance in such circumstances is the logical choice. This is especially true for a band member—as opposed to a solo artist—because your words will reflect on all others in the group.

Speaking of the band he was once a part of, Marshall refuses to comment on his ex-bandmates' views toward all that has transpired. "I haven't really spoken about them," he says. "And I feel like that's not my business to." But for artists in general, Marshall believes they have a particular responsibility to move the audience—which is hard to do when they are self-censoring. "I think, absolutely, it's got to move you. The art's responsibility is to move you. And that can be emotional, it can be literal—if it's music—but it can also be intellectual. And that's absolutely its responsibility. Otherwise, what is it?"

Ultimately, though, Winston doesn't think that artists should be immune from any criticism for their opinions. "In fact, it would be bad if they weren't criticized for their opinions. So I'm not saying that . . . true criticism shouldn't happen, and if parties speak out on difficult issues, they know that that's going to happen. But I do think that we've gone into censorship territories, which means that self-censorship has taken hold." Now, Winston doesn't mean to imply that First Amendment rights are being threatened just yet, but he references what had happened with Joe Rogan and Spotify as an example, where musicians like Neil Young and comedians like Stewart Lee threatened to pull their work from the platform unless it removed Joe Rogan's podcast. "They're saying that their argument was 'we need to take this down because it's misinformation,' but what they're really supporting is a culture of less speech. It's a culture of 'wrong speech shouldn't exist.'" It's worrying for Winston that this is becoming a culture among artists themselves, to deplatform other artists.

He's quick to add, though, that he believes that it's absolutely legitimate for artists like Neil Young to remove their work if they don't support what Spotify is doing. "They [can practice] their freedom of speech by removing their art from that platform if they want, but the difference is that they're saying take him down or take us down." They are not just saying that they are leaving; they are saying that they'll stay if they take him down. "So they're against someone else's free speech. That's the difference. That's like the crux of where it's at. That culture is prevalent amongst artists." And unlike someone successful like a Joe Rogan, who had enough power of his own to keep his deal with Spotify, there are many, many others without any power who have much more to lose. In the context of the music industry alone, there are countless artists who don't have deep pockets or long-lasting careers—artists who are only trying to build up a new career and can't afford to risk it all. Those are the artists who are going to see what's going on and are going to keep their mouths shut because they want to avoid getting into trouble and ruining their career before it even gets started. They don't want to be deplatformed. Aside from a very brave few, most won't rock the boat or really say what they think about an issue. "People who say that cancel culture doesn't exist, what they don't realize is when artists like JK Rowling who can weather the storm [are targeted] . . . although she does get canceled in certain aspects, it's the younger artists and the less successful artists who are self-censoring. And that's [the aspect of] the culture that's so dangerous."

From his experience, Winston feels like he's learned a lot. In fact, he says, "I think something I've learned is the key to life." He continues: "The key to life is to have a close-knit group of people around you who love you deeply, and who can share in your successes and your failures, but also, who don't care about the outside world. And it's just about that inside world. And I think if you've got that core group around, you can weather any storm. That's what the big lesson has been for me."

But ultimately, he argues, it is essential to know that the thing that you're risking everything for is indeed the hill you are ready to die on. If you've made that predetermination, then you're not likely to have regrets because you'll know that you've done the right thing and have lived life according to your own principles.

## Notes

It's worth reading Marshall's own statement on why he left Mumford & Sons and the challenges of navigating political views while being a public person. He recounts his love for the band and its members but also his desire to avoid self-censorship without his band suffering the consequences of his speech. See Marshall, Winston, "Why I'm Leaving Mumford & Sons," *Medium*, June 24, 2021, mrwinstonmarshall.medium.com/why-im-leaving-mumford-sons-e6e731bbc255.

He later wrote a piece in which he commented on the response to his leaving the band and further explained his reasons for doing so. Winston Marshall, "A Quiet Revolution for Our Times May Have Begun," *Spectator*, July 8, 2021, thespectator.com/book-and-art/winston-marshall-quiet-revolution-times-begun.

In an interview originally released in June 2021, Marshall talks to Bari Weiss about why he chose to walk away from his successful band following the aftermath of his tweet: "Why Winston Marshall Left Mumford & Sons." YouTube, video uploaded by *The Free Press* on August 14, 2023, www.youtube.com/watch?v=y395bxz-M1Y.

For Ngo's recounting of the attack on him, see Andy Ngo, "A Leftist Mob Attacked Me in Portland," *Wall Street Journal*, July 2, 2019, www.wsj.com/articles/a-leftist-mob-attacked-me-in-portland-11562109768.

Marshall currently hosts *Marshall Matters*, a podcast that explores taboo issues within the creative industries via interviews with its inhabitants. You can find episodes here: www.spectator.co.uk/podcasts/marshall-matters.

He is also active on X @MrWinMarshall.

# 13 Share and Defend Your Point of View

## The Lessons of John Patrick Shanley

*Your job is to go ahead and have a point of view and defend it and develop it. So all that stuff about what you should or shouldn't say . . . that's outside of what it is to be a true writer.*

*—John Patrick Shanley*

If you're a writer, you've likely heard the following piece of advice: "Kill your darlings"—that is, be willing to sacrifice even your prettiest, wittiest, and most clever piece of prose in the service of telling your overall story better. Writers often fail at this, but there's an even more fundamental piece of advice writers often fail to heed: "Say the things that cannot be said." Following this particular piece of advice, not unlike the first one, is easier said than done. If nothing else, you might not feel completely free to do so. Indeed, there might be any number of reasons a writer will avoid saying what needs to be said, but as John Patrick Shanley, the Oscar-winning screenwriter of *Moonstruck* and the Pulitzer Prize–winning playwright of the Tony-winning drama *Doubt*, says, "It's important for you to go ahead [and do it] anyway. That's your job."

Every writer faces this dilemma at some point: "I'm going to say this thing even though it's going to hurt mom, either because she'll find the language offensive or because it's about her and it's negative, or it's about her husband." But, if you're going to be a writer, you're going to have to be okay hurting not just polite society but also your family, friends, and neighbors. "Your job is to go ahead and have a point of view and defend it and develop it. So all that stuff about what you should or shouldn't say . . . that's outside of what it is to be a true writer—the writer is within a bubble and has to defend it and keep that stuff at bay. A writer is serving the artistic impulse in the unconscious. It is self-generating, but it has to be nurtured, fed, and developed."

Of course, in our daily lives, we may not choose to live quite as freely and may self-censor what we say or choose our words wisely to protect other people's feelings—but in a creative space, there needs to be an opportunity to drop the guard. That's part of being an artist.

Take a writer's room for a television series, for example. Shanley immediately brings up *Succession*, a satirical black comedy-drama HBO series. "I mean, look, if you're in a writer's room for [that] show, you are going to say every reprehensible, unacceptable thing that you can think of as fast as you can and never stop. Oh, my God, you cannot believe the uncensored way that they're talking. Their self-interest, wickedness, shallowness, and soullessness. It's part of what makes it popular." There's no way to write a show like that without being willing to completely drop the idea of self-censorship in the writing room. And yet, in today's environment, not all writers feel like they can do so without repercussions, from complaints to the showrunner or network that might threaten your job to public accusations and lawsuits that will end your livelihood. Where there's a risk of not merely offending someone but also ruining your own career, many writers—especially those who are still building their careers—will simply stay quiet and neuter their words. Due to the subjectivity of offense and the power given to those who claim it, even this is no guarantee of safety or security. Missteps happen. Misunderstandings happen. Maliciousness happens, too. Either way, the work is adversely affected.

Beyond the writer's room, it's also not always easy to predict how audiences will react to your words either. How would Robert Downey Jr.'s hysterical performance in 2008's *Topic Thunder* be perceived today? Can a character's racist or crude behavior be separated from the filmmaker? Serious questions about what actress Maria Schneider endured on set aside, could a film like *Last Tango in Paris* even be made in the aftermath of the "Me Too" movement, with its graphic portrayal of rape? It's hard to imagine that it would be greenlit today. The film has disturbed audiences since its release, and yet it captures something about the human psyche. Is the subject matter now too taboo to explore?

"If you go above a certain level of outrageousness, you're safe," says Shanley. "It's when you kind of voice something that's largely conventional and then fold in one or two things that are objectionable to the bourgeois point of view, then that's when you get in trouble." The audience no longer thinks it's the character saying this but rather the creator, play, or movie. "And if it's something, you know, misogynistic, or something strangely admiring of Hitler, whatever it is, then they're like … that is offensive."

Of course, in the golden age of social media, instead of a thoughtful analysis of why something is offensive or irresponsible, we get many people shouting into the ether. Some of those voices go viral, as outrage is often incentivized by Big Tech's algorithms. Who gets to decide what's offensive? Random people on the Internet? One person whose opinion gets vastly magnified? Professional critics? What about the people who are NOT offended? Do they not have the right to watch something even if others find it offensive?

Who would you allow to determine on your behalf what you should and should not be able to watch? For example, when Netflix employees staged a protest against their own company for releasing Dave Chappell's stand-up comedy special "The Closer," some protestors called for better content warnings and more intersectional content as a remedy for the jokes in the special that they considered transphobic, but others called for the special's complete removal from the platform altogether. Should a handful of activists have the right to determine not only what's offensive but also be given the power to prevent others from judging for themselves?

For Shanley, the answer is obvious, but the question itself misses one key point: offensiveness is often central to good comedy and writing. "Well, you know, [the special]'s supposed to be offensive, that's its job," says Shanley. "I saw the special, and one of the great things about it was that we had something to talk about afterwards. The guy was really throwing some issues on the table with a point of view. And it would be bizarre if I have the exact same point of view that he does, and I don't. But he's saying what he thinks, which is what anybody in a bar would do. And he happens to be an incredibly intelligent and charming guy doing it."

Then there's *South Park*. When Shanley saw the first *South Park* movie, he confesses that he just fell out of his chair laughing: "I thought one of the funniest things I've ever seen in my life was the devil and Saddam Hussein having sex. It was just great." The simple animation, he says, somehow helps. "They're completely fearless. They just do it." At the same time, he says that there's something welcoming and inclusive about *South Park* without being stereotypically politically correct. "It's good-natured, has a good sense of humor, and a joy of being alive. And those are very important things."

When asked if political correctness has a place in art, he simply replies: "No."

There's a fear of offending that runs deep, though, and it has become so difficult to navigate that some broadcasters have even begun resorting to adding "trigger warnings" to programs, like the ones demanded by the "Team Trans" protestors at Netflix, something that Shanley is dismissive of. In June 2020, HBO Max brought back the classic film *Gone with the Wind* after temporarily pulling it off its platform, but it added an introductory disclaimer to provide historical context that plays before the film.

"I don't need context," says Shanley. "That's when you start to infantilize culture, where you take adults and you say, you can't watch this until I warn you about certain things. And that is stooping down, pandering. It's insulting, it's insulting," he trails off. More recently, Ian Fleming's James Bond novels have not only been published with a similar warning but have also been edited to remove racist content, as identified by "sensitivity readers." Six Dr. Seuss books were discontinued in 2021 due to content deemed to contain "racist" and "insensitive" imagery, and a number were edited in 2023 to incorporate "inclusive" language. R.L. Stine's *Goosebumps* series got the same treatment, and the author claimed on social media that no changes were ever shown to him.

"We're in a puritanical era," says Shanley. "There is a new puritanism afoot, no question about it, and it's reflected in these things . . . We are pack animals. And we don't have to be told not to write something or make something in a film; we're part of the zeitgeist, and we're going to naturally do it." He explains that if you look at each era of film, you'll notice certain similarities among the films of each era—whether it's in the style of dress, the vices of the characters, the representation of sexual mores, or the levels of violence. "And it changes all the time. If you go back to the '70s and compare it to now, it's unbelievable."

On top of everything, nowadays, as an artist—and a modern person, you've also got sins of the past to contend with. Say someone is running for city council and they dig up a tweet that the person wrote ten years ago and the contents of that tweet are, well, as Shanley describes it . . . a bit psychotic. "You do have the right to look at that and go, well, on my worst day, I would never write that on a public forum—or in private. And there's plenty of those out there."

Some of those tweets—or even bad jokes in movies—document the evolution of ideas and standards that we once held as a society. And some of them were always abhorrent, of course. But what role does forgiveness play? What if that person has completely changed? If we look at even some of our politicians who appear to be the staunchest supporters of, say, LGBTQ rights, it doesn't take long to find them speaking out against things like gay marriage in the past, or worse.

"You are answerable for your actions," says Shanley. "Let's say you're twenty-five years old and you get drunk and you drive a car and you run over somebody, kill them, get away, and don't report it. And now you're fifty years old and they catch you. And you say, look, I don't even remember the guy when I was twenty-five years old, and I was drunk, and I feel so bad about it. Of course, I'm terribly sorry. It's like, yeah, but you did it, and you're responsible for it." But, admits Shanley, he'd still want to look at each situation case-by-case because people really do change. "I think just about everybody changes. Maybe not philosophically. But actually, they change. So that when a guy says, 'I'm not the person I was at twenty-five, now that I'm fifty, and, in fact, I don't even remember the state of mind at that time,' I would be brought to believe that person."

There is a tendency these days for mobs to descend on individuals and attack them en masse for going against what they believe to be correct social behavior. But, says Shanley, mobs sometimes do good things too. "It could be that everyone turns against somebody who is actually up to no good and [effectively] stops them from being a member of society," he says, citing neo-Nazis as an example. "[They] were denounced and people walked away from them and they became pariahs to a certain degree, and so society was functioning in a way that was probably somewhat cleansing." But, he admits, "that knife has two blades, two sides to it. Mobs always go the other way. If you see a lot of people out in the street, don't go out and join them."

As a writer, Shanley believes that he has to develop all the sides of his personality so that he does not have many inhibitors. This means he has few boundaries, which allows for writing with greater emotion. He cites authors who channeled their feelings into art that could make an impact. Upton Sinclair was horrified by the meat industry, so he wrote *The Jungle*, which caused legislation to be written to clean up the meat industry. Émile Zola wrote *J'Accuse . . . !* to shed light on the injustice of the Dreyfus affair. Charles Dickens wrote about child labor. "Zola was angry, Dickens was angry. Upton Sinclair was angry. And they wrote these [books], and they made things better by doing that because they used their anger to a purpose of social betterment."

Lately, many creatives have faced a particular backlash. Either what they are creating isn't "diverse" enough, or if what they are creating is set in a culture that's not their own, they get blamed for cultural appropriation. It seems like a game with no winners. To that, Shanley responds, "I'm not a social engineer." "Yet," he adds, "you have to know what you're doing." When he wrote his first screenplay, he wrote about the neighborhood that he grew up in, which was segregated. And he started writing black characters. In fact, his first professional production was at a theater that was run by the then-preeminent black director in New York. "They wanted to do my play because they thought I was black because it was a play about the Marine Corps, and half the characters were black and written very credibly [and] I was in the Marine Corps. I was living with a lot of inner-city black guys for two years," he says. They produced that play. "I started off as a black playwright," says Shanley, jokingly, "so when I sort of backtracked into being a white playwright, I was like, I can't stay here for too long. This is New York. What I do has to look like New York. And so I made an effort, film after film and play after play, to include it."

Ultimately, though, a writer has a duty to tell the truth about the world he or she is describing. A true artist knows that what they have to say may get some people upset, but they will say it anyway. "Like I said," says Shanley, "you've got to hurt your mother if you want to be a writer"—or, put another way, you can't self-censor for the sake of what others might think if you want to free your voice.

## Notes

If you're a fan of plays, it's well worth reading some of Shanley's. Some of his most popular with theater fans are "Danny and the Deep Blue Sea," "Italian American Reconciliation," "Savage in Limbo," and "Doubt: A Parable." The latter was also adapted into an Academy Award–nominated film he directed, starring Meryl Streep, Philip Seymour Hoffman, Amy Adams, and Viola Davis. He also wrote *Joe Versus the Volcano*, which he also directed and stars Tom Hanks, and *Moonstruck*, starring Nicholas Cage and Cher, for which he won an Oscar for best original screenplay.

For articles on the James Bond rewrites, the pulling of the Dr. Suess books, the Roald Dahl rewrites, and the edits to the R. L. Stine books, see, respectively, Armani Syed, "The Trouble with the Rewrites to the James Bond Books." Time, September 22, 2023, time.com/6258547/james-bond-books-rewritten; Alison Flood, "Dr Seuss Rockets up US Charts after Books Pulled over Racist Portrayals," *Guardian*, September 22, 2023, www.theguardian.com/books/2021/mar/04/dr-seuss-rockets-up-us-charts-after-books-pulled-over-racist-portrayals; Armani Syed, "Why Rewrites to Roald Dahl's Books Are Stirring Controversy," *Time*, September 22, 2023, time.com/6256980/roald-dahl-censorship-debate; and Armando Tinoco, "Goosebumps Author R.L. Stine Edits Book Series, Changes Mental Health, Weight, Ethnicity References," *Deadline*, March 23, 2023, deadline.com/2023/03/goosebumps-author-rl-stine-edits-book-series-changes-mental-health-weight-ethnicity-references-1235279014.

Shanley is rather fond of sharing whimsical thoughts and images on X @JohnJpshanley and Instagram @johnp.shanley

# 14  Put Yourself in the Shoes of Your Critics

## The Lessons of James Damore

*People need to be able to feel safe and work across differences.*
*If they can't, if they're constantly walking on eggshells,*
*they can't effectively work with others—especially others*
*that they see as potentially different.*

—James Damore

James Damore was just a shy Google engineer who excelled at his job when he made media headlines for writing what has been referred to as the "Google memo" in July 2017. He wrote the memo after attending diversity programs at Google, in which the organizers solicited feedback and shared it on an internal mailing list. In the ten-page document, he objected to the company's core assumptions behind its diversity initiatives and its left-leaning bias. He puts it even more simply: "I went to some programs, and they asked for me to give them feedback, so I gave them feedback." He titled the memo "Google's Ideological Echo Chamber."

According to Damore, Google presented itself as being genuinely very open to feedback, and he drafted and shared the memo in good faith: "I really thought that there were elements of the culture that were harming Google, and I wanted to improve it." One of the areas of the memo to get the strongest attention was Damore's claim that men were better represented in tech than women due to biological differences—namely, that "more men may like coding because it requires systemizing" and "women, on average, have more . . . openness directed towards feelings and aesthetics rather than ideas." He added that women also tend to have more interest in people than things and thus "prefer jobs in social and artistic areas" and that they are "more prone to anxiety" and thus, on average, may be less likely to perform well in stressful tech jobs. He suggested that the workplace can be better adapted to these differences, such as by making positions less stressful, without having to engage in what is popularly called reverse discrimination. Among the practices Damore found discriminatory were those that led to the favoring of people with a certain gender or race, whether in mentoring programs or in hiring practices.

Damore didn't anticipate the reaction that ensued. "I knew that there would be some people that would disagree as [they do] with nearly everything, and [because my memo] was against the status quo, but I definitely didn't anticipate it growing into what it was." When a version of the memo was published by Gizmodo and traveled across social media, controversy and public criticism ensued, though some also praised his arguments—including some academics. Google quickly released a statement saying that the memo advanced a viewpoint that the company did not endorse, promote, or encourage and eventually fired Damore for violating its code of conduct. In turn, Damore filed a complaint with the National Labor Relations Board but later withdrew it. He then filed a class action lawsuit but ultimately ended up pursuing private arbitration against Google. Ultimately, "both parties agreed to end the case," says Damore. "Read into that as you will."

What's particularly interesting is that the lens through which Damore's case was seen was so extreme. Either he was vilified as a misogynistic hater of women, or he was standing up to Google and was absolutely correct. There wasn't much room for nuance or a rational conversation—and the whole incident seemed far more controversial than it perhaps needed to be.

"Part of that, I think, is just the internet and social media and how it has transformed how we think about people from certain political affiliations," says Damore. "If you say, 'Oh, yeah, I think this part was right, or this part was wrong,' then you're automatically ceding ground to the other side, and you are seen as a traitor, and there's just this amalgamation of different traits that we associate with the other side. And so, I think that part of it was that it was seen as sort of a battle that needs to be won rather than something where the truth needs to be determined."

In the media coverage, there was a lot of oversimplification and incorrect parsing of Damore's argument. Some had claimed that he had said that women are not as biologically suited for coding jobs as men—which is not exactly an accurate depiction of his words. "I think there are definitely inaccuracies," he admits. "Part of that is that it was a complicated subject, and people wanted to quickly write articles, and so there was a lot of copy and pasting and just using the same quotes." Sometimes, he'd notice that an article would quote his memo incorrectly, and then another article on a different website would have that same quote wrong. It was the Internet's version of broken telephone. "I'd see whole paragraphs kind of copy and pasted," he says, "and I think that once there is a certain narrative, then it's easier to build on that rather than trying to create your own."

Another part of it is that there's something in certain people that makes them want to have villains out there. "People who are fighting for a certain cause want there to be villains to fight against," he says. "So they are not necessarily going to look too deeply into whether he is really that bad or evil, [or] what was the context of this quote. What was his intention in saying this?" It's easier to have the villain uncomplicated, just bad.

Knowing what he knows now, does Damore regret writing the memo and being shoved into the media circus that ensued? "Oh, it's hard to regret things because so much of my life would be different," he says. He did enjoy his time at Google, though. He got to learn, was paid well, and worked on interesting problems. But the whole experience taught him some valuable lessons. "At the very least," he says, "[it] pushed me out of my comfort zone."

He does think that, in retrospect, he probably would have added some things and removed others from the memo—and there's always the lingering potential of not doing it at all, but then he wouldn't be living the life that he is now and wouldn't know the people that he currently knows, including his girlfriend.

He attributes his lack of reluctance to write the memo in the first place to his own social naivety. As someone on the autism spectrum, he did not fully understand office politics. And as someone with a scientific background and an obsessive mind, he says he approached the subject analytically, rooting himself in academic literature to help find a solution to the two questions at the heart of the problem—specifically, why is there a gap in representation in tech and what, if anything, can help narrow this gap? These two questions, in turn, led him to consider a third question that had been gnawing at him: how could these problems be solved without Google resorting to anything illegal or discriminatory? Based on the prevailing culture at Google, this question weighed heavily on Damore. At the most basic level, he simply wanted to have an open discussion about the issue of representation, which required calling attention to Google's own biases.

What did he learn from his experience? "Just seeing how some of the media works, getting to hear from so many people, and I guess maybe gain some modesty from it all too—the more you know, the more you know that you don't know things." Unlike some, Damore, who has always pretty much spoken his mind, didn't really lose friends during the ordeal. "Anyone that knew me knew who I was and that I'm not like whatever they're painting me as. If you know me, then you also read the whole thing in a different light."

He recalls someone in the media telling him in the midst of the uproar that once people saw him, they'd get a completely different picture of the whole controversy—simply because the way he was being painted was so inaccurate. Damore is soft-spoken and polite, nothing like the arrogant "tech bro" image that might come to mind for someone merely following his media depictions.

Although Google fired Damore rather quickly and he didn't get to witness the aftermath at the company directly, he did get many private messages of support. Part of what made Google such a convenient home for an ideological echo chamber, according to Damore, is that they have a lot of young people who are often recruited right out of colleges where the culture has been shifting dramatically. "They have grown in power very recently, and so there's not necessarily a set tradition on how the company or employees should act. So it may just set the landscape to have them try to lay their own ground, and perhaps pursue moral goals more readily than a more established business because they don't need to be so profit-focused." According to Damore, Google didn't have to focus so much on business goals when he was there because they didn't have much in the way of competition, so instead, it focused on moralistic goals. Meanwhile, if you take "a random grocery store or something, they have a ton of competition, and what they care most about is just the profit margin. While these companies are just printing money."

This choice on Google's part wasn't necessarily a poor strategy. It gave Google an advantage when it came to recruitment. Indeed, it is not uncommon for companies to see this alignment of morals and commerce as a recruiting tool. This was even a consideration for Damore himself. "I did not want to join a lot of different tech companies because I felt like they were a net negative to the world," he says. "I found Google was contributing, and I really liked their motto of just making the world's information universally accessible. There's a lot of talented people that will take a pay cut to join a company with conditions that they believe in."

Another contributing factor that led to the monoculture at Google is that, like many tech companies, it has its own internal social media. This means that it's much easier for echo chambers to be magnified within the company and to cause adverse effects across the company. "I do think that it was a negative for the culture to be so silencing and harassing of particular sections of the company," he says.

The silencing of anyone who questioned the company's particular moral approach was enabled, in large part, by the company's internal social media. When mobs can so easily be formed within companies, many employees with differing opinions might hesitate to speak up altogether. That means that the companies won't hear any counters to their policies. Employees won't question anything. "And you really do need people to question what's happening because . . . somewhat ironically, the diversity things totally backfire in situations where you can't speak your mind. People need to be able to feel safe and work across differences. If they can't, if they're constantly walking on eggshells, they can't effectively work with others—especially others that they see as potentially different."

This can also lead to a more superficial, distanced work environment among colleagues since everyone is afraid of saying the wrong thing. "I remember seeing articles where it [listed] things you can and cannot say in the office," recalls Damore. "And it was being totally serious." The articles essentially said that you can't ask anyone about their personal life or share anything personal. "And it's like, okay, wow, you just never get to know anyone."

One of Google's justifications for firing Damore was that, through his words, he had contributed to creating a culture that was not "work safe," particularly for females, so it was necessary to fire him to protect Google's employees. Of course, any given individual can consider anything unsafe when it comes to words. For Damore, a safe work environment doesn't imply that a company must protect people from words but rather the opposite. "I think one necessary ingredient is the feeling that you can speak your mind without being unfairly judged and where your failures aren't seen as inherent flaws in yourself. Rather, just failures that can be learned from."

When people are afraid to speak their minds, the ideas and attitudes found in the echo chambers that arise, especially those found on social media, do not align with the ideas and attitudes of the broader public. "I never meet people in real life that are like what I see online," says Damore. Within Google's own social media echo chamber, Damore would often see the same five or six people posting the same things and commenting on their own posts. "It was really weird to see that those five people represent so much of the volume of what was online within the company."

Damore also believes that a lot of the counterproductive behavior that we see online is much less common in person and that having more difficult conversations in person might be a better approach: "I think that there's likely techniques to deescalate a conversation, make it less of a battle and more of a discussion. And I think also just asking yourself why you're having a conversation: Is it to try to prove them wrong or is it to understand them better? Is it to change their mind?"

After Damore was fired so publicly from Google, he looked for other work opportunities. He partook in over twenty anonymous interviews, and he passed every single one of them. "But as soon as I got to the stage where I had to give them my name, they wouldn't talk to me at all." Some employment websites even deleted his account. He had to move out of California. He landed at a startup for a while and has been spending time working on game design, learning Spanish, and dabbling in AI. He has some financial independence at this point, and it has afforded him freedom that many do not have. But it's important to remember that he could have just as easily ended up with no means of support.

Since his firing, Damore has been asked to speak on various panels. While participating on a panel at Portland State University with Heather Heying, Peter Boghossian, and Helen Pluckrose, a protester literally attempted to pull the plug on the event by pulling cables on the sound system and breaking an antenna. But Damore has more compassion for the protester than one might think. "If they don't feel like they have a voice, and if they think that I am causing harm and that this is the way to reduce that, in some ways, it's brave of them to do that because they probably got in trouble for doing it. Obviously, I would have preferred them to discuss what they disagreed about, but I think that is also burdening some people with being able to fight the battle on my terms." What he means by this is that some people aren't going to be as skilled or comfortable at debating as others, especially if they are going up against someone who is an expert in their field or someone with a lot of public speaking experience. He's not saying that the protester's approach is necessarily correct, but at the same time, he understands their reasons for doing what they did. "I think it's useful to try to see it from their side."

He uses a more extreme example. What if you were at Hitler's rally and had the opportunity to sabotage equipment so that he could not give his speech? "In retrospect, many people would see that as the morally correct thing to do," he says. "There's no way of debating him or anything." He adds: "No one really sees themselves as Hitler, but [some] may see [others] as something like that."

That's an understatement when hearing many of the accusations that have been thrown rather lightly in today's environment—not just at Damore but at many others, including those who shared the panel stage with him in Portland. It's not uncommon for words like "white supremacist" and "Nazi" to be applied rather loosely. "I think we've built these narratives of being the oppressed group in some way; anyone can identify with some way of being the underdog. And it's that power differential that causes you to try to not play fair, potentially, because there's no way to win if you're the underdog and you're playing fair."

There is certainly a sense that many people see themselves not as underdogs who can persevere no matter the circumstances but rather as victims who can acquire power through their underdog status. "It also releases you from responsibility," says Damore. "Because then there's the implication that you don't have agency in your situation." You are where you are, and you do what you do because you have no other choice.

For his part, Damore is just trying to keep himself honest and curious. His experience has exposed him to a lot of random "culture war" content that he hadn't really paid attention to in the past. He certainly views the media differently, as perhaps anyone who looked deeply into the controversy would, but he doesn't quite see himself as part of the culture war himself and says he feels like the same person he has always been: "It's hard to say how I've really changed. I'm not sure that people necessarily change that much." He got on Twitter (now X) right after the dramatic events of the Google memo unfolded, but "I've kind of backed away from that," he admits. "I don't see it as very productive."

He finds the incentives around the online battles to be unhealthy. For example, if you use Twitter enough, you'll quickly get a sense of which posts will get more interactions—those around controversial topics do well, not the nuanced ones. "It's the ones where you make some strong statement that is uncompromising and aligns with what your followers want. But [that's] not really what I'm going after. I don't think that's improving the world." Not only does it mean that you're only reaching those who are already on your own side—the converted—but it's also worse than that. "Other people will see that tweet, and they'll just see how uncompromising and simple-minded you're being. [There] will be a backfire effect on anyone whose mind you would be trying to change."

Still, Damore holds some hope for the future: "I don't think it needs to hit rock bottom to get better. I think things can just incrementally improve. It's possible."

## Notes

It's worth reading Damore's own essay on his dismissal from Google: "Why I Was Fired by Google," *Wall Street Journal*, August 11, 2017, www.wsj.com/articles/why-i-was-fired-by-google-1502481290.

Gizmodo also published his memo, which received nearly four thousand comments: Kate Conger, "Exclusive: Here's The Full 10-Page Anti-Diversity Screed Circulating Internally at Google." Gizmodo, August 5, 2017, gizmodo.com/exclusive-heres-the-full-10-page-anti-diversity-screed-1797564320.

For more on the Portland State University event, see Helen Pluckrose's informative essay "This Is Why We Need to Talk About Diversity," *Areo Magazine*, March 3, 2018, areomagazine.com/2018/03/03/this-is-why-we-need-to-talk-about-diversity.

In an interview with the *Guardian*, Damore expresses how his autism makes it difficult for him to understand how his words will be interpreted. "My biggest flaw and strength may be that I see things very differently than normal," he told his interviewer. "I'm not necessarily the best at predicting what would be controversial." See Paul Lewis, "'I See Things Differently': James Damore on His Autism and the Google Memo," *Guardian*, November 17, 2017, www.theguardian.com/technology/2017/nov/16/james-damore-google-memo-interview-autism-regrets.

You can find more about his current work at jamesdamore.com. He's on X under @JamesADamore.

# 15 Have a Plan B

## The Lessons of Katie Herzog

*What's integral about being human is this idea that
we can express what's coming out of our brains.*

*—Katie Herzog*

Katie Herzog worked as a freelance journalist writing for *The Stranger*, a snarky, iconoclastic, very left-leaning weekly in Seattle. The sort of place where a controversial article about something people are talking about would generally go over well. But that's not really what happened when Herzog wrote an article about trans people who either halted or reversed their transitions. "There was very much a backlash within the paper over the piece," she recalls. She expected that some people were going to be mad about it, but she couldn't imagine the scale. "I knew almost intuitively that this issue was toxic," she says, "But I didn't know that this was going to haunt me for the next [five] years. But you know, if I could go back and tell myself: 'You're going to write this one article—5,000 words are going to change your life forever—I don't know if I would have done it."

She reconsiders: "I might have?" In a hypothetical scenario in the moment, she's not sure. There's a 50/50 chance. But, knowing what she knows now, she's glad she did it. But at first, she wasn't quite so certain. When the article came out, she wasn't exactly beloved by those she considered to be her people. She says that most of the direct hate and denouncements happened online, including by people she'd been very close to. "Somebody is more likely to dive into the bushes to avoid me than to confront me in person," she says." In addition to hate mail, some angry residents burned stacks of the paper containing her article and sent her a video of it. Others posted stickers around town calling her a transphobe and a Nazi sympathizer. Someone put graffiti across the door of *The Stranger*. She lost friends. She was hesitant to share her name with people she'd meet while out. She was no longer welcome in her long-time local gay bar—where someone took a picture of her Twitter avatar and put it in the urinal. In fact, she wasn't welcome in her adoptive city. Eventually, she moved out to a small town across the water, where she could buy a home with her wife.

"At the time, it was very difficult," she recalls. When the article first came out, she says, she had lunch with Dan Savage, and they both expressed surprise that the article hadn't made much of a stir. But by the time Herzog got home, she says, that all changed. Her name was everywhere. That weekend, she attended a nonbinary wedding of her wife's friends: "I felt like everybody fucking knew and somebody said something . . . and I went and hid in the car and smoked weed by myself."

She admits that she didn't quite realize the outcry from her piece was going to be so bad because she believed the fact that she's a lesbian—who at the time identified as queer—would soften the criticism somewhat. "I was totally wrong about that," she says. If anything, it made it worse because it made her the "heretic person within the tribe."

Although losing friends wasn't the easiest thing, the endless awkward interactions—constantly wondering what people are thinking or what they know about her—are less of a concern for her today. Herzog has adopted a particular attitude that has greatly helped her: "Look, people who know me, know me. And I've always sort of felt like I care about the opinions of people I respect and love. And I don't really care about the opinions and people I don't. It's taken a long time to get to this place. And age is probably a huge part of it. But that served me very well."

She admits, however, that there's probably some detriment there, too, because she might miss some good criticism from time to time by writing people off. But, she says, in terms of self-preservation and not crumbling in the face of thousands of people calling you awful things, it's valuable. This allows her to continue to be vocal on social media, but, as part of her self-preservation, she limits her Twitter notifications. "There's literally thousands of people on both sides of the political spectrum telling me shit. I can't see any of it, so it frees me to say whatever the fuck I want because I shut off the noise." Again, she admits there's danger there because it also means she may not be getting much-needed criticism, but it also enables her to be free with her words. "What people are mad about is not you," she explains. "They are mad about a cartoon version of you that doesn't exist."

The irony is that for as much negative attention as Herzog received for her piece on detransitioners, it was the most-read article she'd ever written and ultimately led to some positive professional outcomes. *The Stranger* ended up hiring her as a full-time staff writer—a position she left in March 2020, volunteering to take a furlough as the paper took a financial hit during the pandemic. "There's no way that I would probably be hired by any sort of left-leaning paper in America right now," says Herzog.

In her last post for them, she wrote: "Since joining *The Stranger* in 2017, a lot of people have called for me to be fired. From my piece on detransitioners to my skepticism of #MeToo, I've rubbed many of you fine (and not-so-fine) readers the wrong way. *The Stranger*, despite all the takes I've had, has stuck by me throughout. Now it's my time to give back by helping the company keep costs down."

Although the furlough was expected to last eight weeks, she never returned.

But Herzog found something that so many in her position are not so fortunate to secure—complete independence. "I answer to nobody," she says. Today, she runs a popular podcast called *Blocked and Reported* with her cohost, fellow journalist Jesse Singal. "I can say whatever I want; I'm totally free," she declares. But, she's quick to admit, "most people aren't."

She recognizes that her life could have gone on a completely different path and how incredibly lucky she is to have things turn out the way they did. Her first big feature for *The Stranger* was about microdosing acid for a month. "I could have gone on writing pieces like that, writing these columns, and writing about the news," she says, "and I would probably be working there now." But instead, she wrote this one piece, and it changed everything. There are all these people who tried to cancel her, and yet, she says, it has done nothing but help her. "[But] that's not the case for everybody, for sure," she acknowledges. "I think I'm very lucky in this respect. Socially, it definitely made my life more difficult, but professionally, it's only helped me." Personally, she says, "Just speaking from my own experience, I would say that I have made as many friends as I've lost, but most of them are not in-person, and that's difficult because [we] need community and gaining friends on the internet doesn't quite replace that . . . I've certainly benefited on a professional level and less on a personal level."

Herzog compares her financial freedom to the "Bernie Sanders model of funding." Instead of having one overlord who pays her salary, she now has thousands of people who help her pay her bills by giving very small amounts. "It just makes it a lot easier to become free." If you piss off your employer, you might lose your job. If you upset one person, they might stop their $5 donation. This is the model that allows her to truly be free to say what she wants to and cover the kinds of stories that she'd like.

There are many topics today that make us feel like we're navigating a classic game of Minesweeper, but few seem quite as loaded with traps as trans issues. "Part of it is that it takes up a bigger place in society because [while] we're talking about a small number of people, we're talking about policy changes that impact a wide number of people. So if you're talking about something like self-ID, bathroom policies, or whatever, this might only, on its surface, impact the trans population, but really, it impacts women in particular. So that is a niche issue that really has wider implications, including the redefining of what sex is, which is hugely, hugely important for society."

The discussion around the idea of changing sex or gender has evolved considerably in recent years. If nothing else, trans rights are something that is being taken seriously, whereas before, scant attention was paid to the issue. "We're talking about a small population, people who were basically treated with jokes as clowns until recently, and so there is a real human rights issue here."

Part of this attention is due to the success of the gay rights movement, says Herzog. "You get organizations like the Human Rights Campaign, which pivoted away from gay marriage in 2015," explains Herzog. "After that passing in the Supreme Court, we had all this funding, and so they have to pivot to something." So, they pivoted to trans issues. Herzog says that she's only aware of one gay rights organization that was devoted to marriage equality that shut down after that goal was achieved. "That's it, everyone else pivoted," she explains. "Part of that is just self-protection. You have jobs, you have a giant budget, you've got to do something. What's next on the list?"

What started as a fight to protect trans people from discrimination in jobs and housing has morphed into a push to include trans women in all-female spaces, whether in prisons, changing rooms, or sports. "There's all these downstream effects that in some ways, I think, will ultimately end up hurting trans people. I think most people believe that you shouldn't be kicked out of your house for being trans. Are most people going to believe that a trans [woman should] play on a woman's soccer team? That's a different question. So it's pushing the boundaries." When it comes to things like sports, bathrooms, prisons, and other women's spaces, it's a more delicate situation because it means having to balance some people's rights against other people's rights. For many, supporting this agenda has become a way of signaling how progressive someone is. "It's become this sort of market in the cultural war where if you're on this one particular side, you're on the right side of history—and that's often how the media portrays it, but that's not really true. And I don't think it represents, at least in the U.S., the majority of Americans who probably don't believe that." Even among trans people, there's not necessarily a consensus on many of the issues affecting them, but only certain voices get access to the megaphone that's known as the media, giving a false impression.

The sharp rise in trans-identified individuals has also raised questions. Is this a natural outcome of increased acceptance, or are other forces at play? Herzog points to the idea of "social contagion," whereby many younger individuals with no history of gender dysphoria have suddenly come out as trans. For those individuals in particular, it suggests social media and media coverage have been powerful forces. "It's very multifaceted," says Herzog, but I think there were convergences that have made this a major issue within our culture right now. Media has a huge part to do with it."

There's no denying that Herzog is part of a fortunate group of people who have been able to find both freedom and a measure of success in being able to speak about controversial topics. Many people point to those like her as an example of the nonexistence of the suppression of freedom of expression, or they might even accuse people like her of being "grifters" who don't believe what they say but who are simply trying to monetize hot-button topics.

"I'm the exception to this rule," she answers. "I'm not the rule . . . I have absolutely benefited from cancel culture, which is one of the ironies of it. But most people haven't; they've suffered from it. People who are like adjunct professors or working in PR or working at a lighting company or whatever. And those are the people we should be concerned about."

Herzog says that she gets many messages from people seeking advice about their own situations or even just wanting to share with someone who's been through a similar experience. Most people, when they become targets, are silenced. Most people aren't easily able to support themselves or continue to speak out after their careers and reputations have been destroyed by the mob. "The issue is people who don't have a fucking voice," she says. "Nobody is going to really cancel J. K. Rowling. She might sell fewer books. Probably not."

There's little doubt, however, that attacks on J. K. Rowling and other high-profile people have had a chilling effect overall. If nothing else, "this stifles dissent, it stifles conversation, and makes it harder to say things that are true, which is bizarre and unhealthy for any culture."

What might be unhealthy for the culture might be a good survival strategy for the individual, however. "People need to be realistic and evaluate where they are in life," warns Herzog. "So if you are an untenured professor, you have three kids, and the likelihood of you getting another job is minimal, be really careful before you speak up. And I hate to say that, but don't let your passion outweigh your material obligations. But for people who go through that process and judge that they can stand to lose something, realize that you're not alone. And I know it's incredibly cliché to say, but it's a wide community of people who feel the same way and feel passionate about this, and you can connect with them. And that will be helpful. But it's really difficult. Some people will benefit; some people will suffer. It kind of depends on what you're doing in life, and you should be able to evaluate that and figure out what's right for you and what's not."

For those who are willing to risk their own reputation or livelihood for their principles, she says, "Make sure you have a plan B."

Despite her hard-earned financial independence, Herzog says she still self-censors on occasion, especially in social situations—but she has far less fear than she did when she had a "real" job. Somebody recently asked her what the point of being independently funded is if she can't talk about whatever she wants. "And that sort of gave me a baby kick in the pants."

To Herzog, it's essential that we discuss all ideas, including the ones that she disagrees with. If nothing else, it may lead us to make better decisions. "What's integral about being human is this idea that we can express what's coming out of our brains," she says. "I don't think that government should be able to impinge that—I don't think that companies should be able to infringe that . . . You improve society by figuring out what's real—figuring out how things work. You can't improve society if you just suppress the views that you don't like."

But remember, keep a contingency plan in your back pocket and try to make yourself earthquake-proof—just in case your world starts falling apart.

## Notes

A good introduction to Herzog's work is, of course, the article that set her world on fire: Katie Herzog, "The Detransitioners: They Were Transgender, Until They Weren't," *Stranger*, June 28, 2017, www.thestranger.com/features/2017/06/28/25252342/the-detransitioners-they-were-transgender-until-they-werent.

She also responded to the uproar over the piece here: "A Response to the Uproar Over My Piece, 'The Detransitioners,'" *Stranger*, July 3, 2017, www.thestranger.com/lgbtqitslfa/2017/07/03/25262759/a-response-to-the-uproar-over-my-piece-the-detransitioners.

Herzog and her cohost of *Blocked and Reported*, Jesse Singal, discussed left-wing cancel culture on *Reason Podcast* on June 17, 2020. It's available at reason.com/podcast/2020/06/17/katie-herzog-and-jesse-singal-on-left-wing-cancel-culture.

The *New York Times* covered Herzog's experiences in a piece on how people who have been "canceled" sometimes end up building a community together after their experiences push them together. John McDermott, "Those People We Tried to Cancel? They're All Hanging Out Together," *New York Times*, November 2, 2019, www.nytimes.com/2019/11/02/style/what-is-cancel-culture.html.

In addition to her popular *Blocked and Reported* podcast (blockedandreported.org), she's a prolific X user @kittypurrzog.

# 16 Be Willing to Fight

## The Lessons of Jodi Shaw

*It was scary because it felt like I have just launched a tiny pebble up at Goliath. How is he going to respond?"*

*—Jodi Shaw*

Jodi Shaw loved her job as a children's librarian at the Brooklyn Public Library, but she needed to relocate after a divorce. She and her ex wanted to find an affordable area where they could live in proximity for the sake of their two kids. A long-time singer-songwriter, Shaw has always considered herself "super, super liberal—like to an extreme," so she was excited about moving back to Northampton, Massachusetts—which she describes as being a super liberal, funky, and anything-goes-kind of town. Having lived there as a student at Smith College, this seemed like a good place for the move. Smith immediately began to look for work.

Shaw was excited to receive an offer to be a temporary librarian at Smith. "The reason they hired me was my demonstrated ability to engage patrons in a creative, fun, out-of-the-box manner," she recalls. "I was an engagement librarian. I was also doing some instruction. And so, I was tasked with creating a highly engaging orientation for first-year students. Apparently, the year before it had been a disaster, and they were really hoping I could, like, do something great." Her goal was to join the library as a permanent staff member, so she wanted to make a good impression. She knew it would help her case for a position that had just opened up. "In fact, I pitched and created the position that was basically like a position doing what I was already doing," she says.

Shaw learned that the orientation slot she had been assigned was on the last day of a multiday event and late in the day. Although the event was mandatory for students, it was hard enough to get them to attend events earlier in the schedule. She was, therefore, encouraged to do something "wild and crazy" and was told a push would be made to get first-year students to attend the presentation. Shaw knew that she had to do something really impressive. "So I left her office, and I'm thinking, what am I going to do? Geez, I just made a big promise . . . It became apparent to me very quickly that it's a question of how I transmit a bunch of otherwise very boring information to a bunch of eighteen-year-olds who are exhausted in a fun, engaging manner where they're not going to be, you know, sleeping." Since Shaw had a musical background, the answer seemed obvious to her. She'd write and perform some kind of song. She settled on a rap.

She spoke to her supervisor about her idea. The supervisor was a bit nervous about a middle-aged white librarian performing a rap, so Shaw sent her a link to a rap video she had previously done for a contest when she was in library school. It had won first place. Her supervisor's response? "Okay, now I get it. This could be really good." The supervisor approved the project and drew up a budget. Shaw spent all of that summer working on it. Shaw had a huge committee of people all across campus involved in it. She also hired a crew to do sound and lighting. "I mean, it was like I was going all out with a full blessing of the department and the Dean of Libraries." She was only mildly concerned when her supervisor was replaced that summer. Her new supervisor also became the head of the search committee for the position she hoped to be offered.

About a month before her presentation was supposed to take place, an incident occurred on campus that put people on edge. A white janitor in his 60s and with poor eyesight had called campus police to report a black student who had been eating in a dining hall on campus. This caused a big ruckus. The student wrote on her Facebook page: "All I did was be Black. It's outrageous that some people question my being at Smith College, and my existence overall as a woman of color."

The ACLU got involved, and the college apologized to the student, put the janitor on paid leave, and began to institute policies and initiatives to eliminate "implicit bias" at the school. They introduced training and planned campuswide conversations—before they'd even investigated what had actually happened.

So here was Smith, a month after that incident, about to do this huge performance with only six days to spare. Her new supervisor comes into her office and tells her that she will no longer be able to do this presentation. "I said, 'Why not?' And he said: 'Because you're white.' Those are the words he used." Understandably, Shaw was shocked. "He cited the incident of July 31. He cited that as the need to be sensitive." She asked him whether she'd be able to go ahead with the presentation if she wasn't white. He responded, "Yes." "He didn't even hesitate."

She was confused. "I was like, wait a minute, that seems like racial discrimination to me." At the same time, she understood that if she were to voice that out loud or complain, in that environment, that would be taken as a clear indication that "[I'm] obviously a white supremacist," she half-jokes. Shaw was conflicted. Should she report this? She was still being considered for a permanent job. If she reported this situation, she feared that everyone would think she's a racist and that she wouldn't get hired. "I didn't want to jeopardize my [job]," she recalls, "and also there was part of me that was like, am I racist? Was this not racist? Because I'm white? The manner in which they did it—it was so matter-of-fact. They put [it] in an email. They didn't even try to hide it. I mean, it was like, 'Clearly, we're denying your professional opportunity because of your skin color, but we're not even going to bother hiding this because we assume it's totally fine. So that was that was like a gaslighting thing."

Convinced that she wouldn't get hired anyway, Shaw withdrew her job application.

"I thought this environment is so toxic and messed up. I'm not going to get hired anyway. I've already been humiliated. I've been accused of being culturally insensitive, so I'm leaving." So, she got a job elsewhere on campus and started working there. Her new job at Residence Life, she thought, was below the radar. There, she dealt with very practical things like handing out student keys and ID cards. But turns out that even Residence Life departments were actually notorious for being "little social justice factories," says Shaw. "I soon found out . . . these people who work in Residence Life, a lot of them . . . get their master's degree in higher education. And those programs are so social justice infused, it's really just like a training academy for social justice activism." When they go to work in colleges like Smith, they begin to infuse their activism into the residential curriculum at the houses and residence halls. While the purported intent is to help students develop life skills and self-aware-ness, "it's all based on social justice," says Shaw. "You're going to figure out your identity by first figuring out what your skin color is, your gen-der, what's your sexual orientation, instead of, like, doing the hard work of actual identity development. And it's a period of time when students are really finding out who they are. They're actually being squashed and reduced [into identities] when they should be expanding themselves and discovering their inner lives and their complexities."

Shaw was disappointed at what she was seeing, but she needed the job, so her attitude overall was, "Go for it. My job is to give out keys and IDs. I'm just going to do my job, and you guys do your thing." The prob-lem is, they wouldn't just let her do her job. "They just kept pushing, and they kept saying, 'You have to help us create this curriculum, this space of social justice.' And I was like, 'I'm really uncomfortable with that.'"

What made her most uncomfortable with the curriculum was actually its effects on students of color. "I thought it was fairly disempowering to all students because, like I said, it's reducing them and squashing them and putting them in boxes. But especially to students of color, there was this overarching message of 'you are so oppressed and powerless, and please let us know you're going to need extra help, and we're here to help you.' I mean, this messaging was infused in everything, and it was really disturbing to me."

Shaw thinks people should be encouraged to talk about any issues they might have, but she felt like the whole approach felt rather scripted. There was a specific filter through which the complexity of people's lives had to be talked about and distilled. It felt condescending and belittling to students, and she didn't want to be a part of that, so she started pushing back gently—talking about the notion of anti-fragility and suggesting a trauma-informed lens. She gently sought to introduce another lens into the programming that didn't reduce people to their skin colors or political abstractions, but she didn't get far. "They were definitely on the social justice path," she says. And she had to go to workshops and discussions where they'd discuss identity and gender and other such things. "I would mostly remain silent," she recalls. "Just wouldn't participate." Over time, she began to push back more.

She started to think more about what happened in the library. Wasn't what happened illegal? "It's illegal to ask about your sex or your race or any other protected characteristic in a job interview. Why is it a continued condition of my employment to do so? So I got that in my head. And I was like, yeah, this is wrong."

Around this time, Shaw was told that she had to attend a mandatory work retreat. During it, the facilitators went around the room and asked participants to talk about their understanding of their race in the context of their childhood. That was the final straw for Shaw. "Those are two things I don't want to talk about at work," she says. Knowing that race would be a subject that would be brought up during the retreat, Shaw approached her director a month before and told her that she was not comfortable discussing her race at work. "There was no pushback at all. She just said, 'Oh, well, then, just say that at the workshop.'" Shaw ended up attending the retreat and remained a bit nervous, but the director was there. She hoped he would back her up and things would be okay. As everyone went around and spoke their piece, it was Shaw's turn. So, as agreed previously, she told them that she didn't feel comfortable contributing in that way. "At first, it seemed okay," she recalls. "But then later the facilitators were like, 'The person that said that is enacting a power play. It's an act of aggression.' It's white fragility."

In a perhaps misguided attempt to empower some people, there has been this ideological shift that seems to focus on forcing white people to acknowledge their racism—or at least some level of guilt. Often, this means not allowing white people to take responsibility for their achievements without admitting their privilege. "According to this ideology, any achievement is simply because of your white skin, and you didn't actually have anything to do with it," explains Shaw. She views it as something that's very harmful. "It's postmodernism gotten mad."

Shaw admits that she's not an academic, but given her experiences in an academic setting, she has spent a lot of time thinking about why this has happened. She has also spent a long time just trying to figure out why she herself went along with it for as long as she did. Why didn't she pay more attention? Why are other people going along with it without raising any questions? Why is this happening in our culture? And most importantly, what makes a person wake up to what's going on?

It led her to think a lot about brainwashing and cults, too.

But as she grappled with these thoughts, it was clear to her that her mental state was not in good shape. The damage being done by not speaking out about what was happening was slowly eating at her. "It was horrible. I could see that the psychic damage was going to far outweigh any damage I might cause by coming out."

Any hesitation she might have had was squashed by that workshop. "After that workshop, I thought, gee, now I can't even just keep my head down and my mouth shut. I literally have to say words that they want me to say. This is now compelled speech. This isn't suppressed speech. This is compelled speech. That is the line for me. Somehow, that was the line." She couldn't even go into a room and stay silent because that would be interpreted as an act of aggression.

Since those pushing this programming at Residence Life couldn't be reasoned with, she decided to pay a visit to the person in charge of the school's compliance with the Civil Rights Act. "She looked at me like she couldn't believe [what I saw saying]." Then she asked: "Do you believe in white privilege?" She continued to explain that the Civil Rights Act of 1964 was created to protect traditionally marginalized groups of people. "Which I interpreted to mean, not white people," says Shaw. It was then explained to her that if she proceeded with filing a complaint, they'd have to hire an outside investigator. Shaw asked: "Aren't you the person that investigates these claims?" To which she responded: "Yeah, normally I am, but you're white. So it's different." Shaw took that to mean that her claim would not be taken seriously. "She said that twice, and she put it once in an email. This is how bold [it is]. It's almost like the law doesn't even exist for them anymore. So that was not encouraging." But Shaw proceeded to type up a complaint.

At the same time, Shaw's father was dying from cancer, so it was a difficult time. Between the library incident, the workshop experience, the complaint, and her father's illness, it was tough. Shaw finally turned in the complaint in May 2020. Two weeks later, her dad died.

That same month, George Floyd was killed. Protests broke out everywhere. The pandemic led to staff furloughs, and the summer of racial reckoning led Smith College to prioritize new racial justice initiatives. "They had this big committee working on all this stuff. They had sent this letter [saying] we're going to make sure people are being paid equitably across registers of social identity, like all this language, I didn't even know what that meant." Smith noticed words she hadn't come across before: "All of a sudden, there's this new language. There's a lot of new words, and I was getting invited to go to white-only staff meetings where staff can contemplate their privilege." If she had been walking on eggshells in what she saw as a hostile environment before, this was even worse. Shaw viewed this as racial segregation.

Shaw started emailing people and having meetings. Then Smith released a big document saying it would institute a number of measures and employees would be held accountable. "This sounds pretty serious," says Shaw. "I'm going to be held accountable." She reached out to the director of the college's equity and inclusion office. Shaw asked: "What do these words mean? What is antirace? What does equity mean? And he couldn't explain it to me. And then he said, you know, 'Maybe you should read *How to Be an Anti-Racist* by Ibram X. Kendi.'" She asked whether that was an official Smith College HR book that she must read as an employee.

"How can I be held accountable when you don't even know what you're talking about?" she asked herself. Still, she had hope as she awaited a response to her complaint: "I thought, surely, if I send reasonable requests for definitions and clarity [and] they investigate my complaint, which is very thorough and is backed up by lots of document evidence, surely they will see how horrible this is and how horribly the employees were treated."

But as she kept waiting for word on her complaint, things were only getting crazier on campus, and it didn't seem like anyone was listening to common sense. Shaw thought it might be time for a different approach, so she created some social media pages, just in case she was going to have to go with the nuclear option: making a YouTube video.

The breaking point was when she was called into a meeting to talk about a racial justice document. She thought she had made it quite clear that she had no interest in going into any further meetings about race. "Everyone in my department has been told now that I'm committing an act of aggression if I don't talk about race." And yet, this meeting was mandatory. She was so anxious she had hives. "I was like: I can't go to this meeting. I can't go to this meeting."

So she made a YouTube video, and it went viral. "And then my whole world changed." She went on Tucker Carlson a week later and was put under investigation—her appearance was brought up as proof that she's a white supremacist.

When Shaw went with, as she calls it, "the nuclear option," she wasn't sure what to expect. Either she would release the video and it would fizzle out into nothing, or, well, *something* would happen. Either way, adrenaline flowed as she waited for the initial impact. "It was scary because it felt like I [had] just launched a tiny pebble up at Goliath. How is he going to respond? I was like, 'Holy shit, like, what's going to happen now?'" If nothing else, she assumed she would receive a lot of hate online. "I thought, well . . . I just won't look at the computer." To her surprise, the overwhelming majority of incoming messages were positive. Most of the hostility she ended up encountering was from those affiliated with Smith College, including students and alums. Things were particularly tense when she was under investigation. "They said my colleagues felt harmed by your videos. If you watch my videos, they're very mild."

When they concluded their two-months-long investigation into her, they found no fault whatsoever. "It was total bullshit."

Shortly thereafter, she retained counsel and filed a racial discrimination and retaliation lawsuit against the school. She says that she wanted to amicably resolve the situation, but things got a bit convoluted during settlement negotiations. "In the end, they did offer me something very generous. That was hard for me. I had to think really hard about it. I mean, I was in my shower, crying. I couldn't because I would have had to sign a nondisclosure agreement, and I just knew I would regret it." She declined. "And they were like, 'Oh, okay, well, then I guess you can come back to work then.'" Smith felt like it would have been a bit like going back to an abusive partner: "If I go back, I can continue to fight, but they're going to be watching every move I make . . . they are going to fire me the first [chance they get]. I didn't have tenure, and I knew it was going to be so hostile, so distracting—it would be hard for me to do my work." Ultimately, she decided not to return to Smith College.

Bari Weiss published her resignation letter, and the story exploded, as did her GoFundMe. A few days later, Michael Powell wrote a story for the *New York Times* about Shaw's situation, and the media coverage continued from there. Not only were people interested in Shaw's story, but they were also excited to share their own stories with her. "And so I started engaging with some of these people," she recalls. "There were so many of them, and their stories were really heartbreaking." There was a woman who lost the opportunity to have fertility treatments. Another woman lost her job twice. "Just these stories of the very real material impact [on] people who'll just innocently step into this huge trap, and their whole leg gets cut off. And it's heartbreaking. It just shows you how damaging and destructive this fever is."

Shaw says that some people think that we are going to be able to successfully push back on all of this and go back to the way things were. She doesn't think that this is ever going to happen, but she sees more people speaking up than before. She admits that she's also had some fears about talking to certain people or being associated with the right, particularly when networks like Fox would invite her on to do interviews. People would reach out to her and tell her that they support her message but ask her, "Couldn't you go on CNN instead?" Aside from the fact that more left-leaning networks aren't so welcoming when it comes to Shaw's story, there's something else she had to grapple with. "For some reason, people in this fear being associated with the right. That's something I had to struggle with. I was afraid to talk to certain people. I was very worried about my image, and now I can see that that's all just clearly bullshit and that I was really buying into this thing and having all this fear . . . I think that hurts leftists or former leftists because it takes away our power because we're bridled by fear or kind of shackled, like we can't, with an open heart, reach across the aisle and join forces with a group of people who would very much be allies."

Shaw points out that this is not a policy debate about issues like universal health care or abortion—it is about authoritarianism or totalitarianism versus liberal democracy. "Either you're actively pushing against it or you're complying."

She understands that people have real reasons to comply. No one wants to lose their job, for example—including her. But she sees this as only the beginning. "If this keeps going, it's going to be more than a job [that we lose]."

Sometimes you have to look under the rug and see all the dirt that you don't want to look at, says Shaw. You can't avoid it forever. She recalls what someone once told her about the Chinese Cultural Revolution—that only 5 to 8 percent of the population believed in the ideologies that were being forced down. Everyone else just went along with it out of fear. On the other end, she says, there were [only] around 5 percent of the population who were actively fighting it. Maybe even as little as 3 percent. "I used to think it can't just be three." But now, after everything she's gone through and experienced, she says, "I think it's three or less."

Despite common conceptions, totalitarianism isn't necessarily a top-down endeavor. Once a sufficient percentage of the population is effectively self-policing, then the conditions for a totalitarian regime have been met. "And I think the conditions have been met."

Shaw describes the inability to stand down in the face of what she views as wrong as almost a "defect" or perhaps a "genetic mutation" in her. She can't help it. "Sometimes I wish I could," she confesses. "Maybe it would be more comfortable. But yeah, it's like an inability to tolerate bullshit. It's an inability to tolerate falsities. I mean, I can tolerate them to an extent, but also—injustice—seeing it and being asked to participate in it? I mean, that's a real line. Like, okay, I guess I can stomach it if you're over there doing it—I'm queasy. But now you're asking me to participate in it with you? No way. Yeah, I think it's like a defect or something."

For Shaw, to not say anything is a kind of a lie. "It's like you're saying you're okay with it or something." She believes the solution is to create a parallel culture in the face of what's becoming increasingly totalitarian. She sees this happening already. "I think that networks are very important. Really investing time in the people around you and building your relationships, [people] you can count on and rely on."

Shaw believes that there are two distinct worlds now. One world is aware of what's going on in both worlds, but the other is stuck in a bubble. There are two veins of information flowing, two societies, but one group has access to only one—or at least chooses to see only that one. "And I think that's a real problem."

At some point, the two worlds will have no choice but to collide. They cannot avoid this forever. She recalls the racial incident at the dining hall, the one that led to her orientation program being canceled and caused her to start thinking and speaking up about these issues. Although media outlets like the *New York Times*, *Washington Post*, and CNN were quick to pick up the initial story, they paid far less attention to the findings of the investigation that followed. In the end, no evidence of bias or racism was uncovered. Turned out that this particular dining space was off-limits and closed for the summer. Whoever was working in the dining room knew the student and allowed her to come in. "The building was shut down, the janitor saw a pair of legs through a glass door, and did what he was told to do, which is if you see something, don't mess with the person, just call campus police. So that's what he did. It turned into a huge fiasco." And ultimately, it was the custodial worker who paid the price regardless of guilt.

As this and so many other cases demonstrate, when truth collides with fiction, the truth inevitably prevails—but only if we're all living in the same reality.

## Notes

On December 25, 2020, Shaw put up a video on YouTube titled "Destruction of the Moral Compass." In it, she talks about some of her experiences getting caught up in Smith College's attempts to combat racism: youtu.be/4WVkj-ikypQ?si=lAyvtWXeddKC7c5R.

For coverage of the story in the *New York Times*, see Michael Powell, "Inside a Battle Over Race, Class and Power at Smith College," *New York Times*, February 24, 2021, www.nytimes.com/2021/02/24/us/smith-college-race.html.

The *Free Press* included Shaw's resignation letter from Smith in a piece by Bari Weiss, "Whistleblower at Smith College Resigns Over Racism," February 19, 2021, www.thefp.com/p/whistleblower-at-smith-college-resigns.

Her website is jodishaw.com and she's also on X: @Smith_Surge.

# Conclusion: No Apologies

When I first went through my own experience struggling to free my voice, I was so anxious and so desperate for advice that I reached out anonymously to a rather famous public figure whose own experience against the outrage mob was well-documented. To my surprise, he was kind enough to write back to me, a complete stranger—a stranger who, at the time, was too terrified to even use her real name. His advice was to hold my ground and hone my arguments. "Generally, any flurry of discontent that emerges because an opposing view emerges only lasts about two weeks, so if you can hold out that long, you may well win," he wrote. Two weeks later, I discovered he was right. People really do have rather short attention spans. They quickly move on to the next target.

But even before I was under fire, I was already struggling with a guilty conscience. I was unhappy with my own inability to speak freely and express what I believed to be true. He advised that I go on the offensive, carefully and strategically, and actively oppose policies that don't align with my values—particularly those who suppress my willingness to speak. "It's hard to know what you think if you're afraid to speak, and it's hard to see how that can be good, assuming that thinking is useful," he wrote. "It's going to be necessary for you to take stock of where you believe you are most dissatisfied with betraying yourself, as you mentioned, and decide how much long-term misery there is going to be in that, compared to the short-term distress of having to make your views known. It's trouble either way. You just get to choose the trouble."

But he gave me some practical words of caution, too. He advised me to put my CV in order and start looking, tentatively, for other job opportunities in other fields. After all, speaking up is not for the faint of heart! It isn't without its risks. It shouldn't be, but it is. The truth is that in my own situation, I likely could have submitted for the sake of professional and personal peace. I could have crafted a narrative that would have allowed me to return to the "in-group." I could have caved. I could have simply allowed the storm to pass me by. But I chose to speak up, and I continued to do so. I did so because not only did I know that I wasn't wrong and I was rather stubborn about that idea, but also because I felt like, in a way, I was speaking up for all of those who are too afraid to speak or are unable to do so. All the people who, for one reason or another, are not yet prepared to take the risk and are living with their silence and, often, with their shame. I owed no apologies to the people who had behaved reprehensibly toward me nor to the many others who had been coerced into compliance.

Not that there is anything wrong with apologizing when an apology is warranted. But no one has the right to demand one when it's not—and no one has the duty to give one. This is a principled position as much as a practical one. For the blind mob, an apology is often perceived as a sign of weakness to be exploited, just as sharks will be quick to attack at the first sign of blood. Indeed, there are many public apologies that have resulted in further agony for the ones offering them, particularly in those cases when no wrong deserving of apology had been committed. If there's one common lesson among all those interviewed for this book, it's this: *don't* apologize if you know you've done nothing wrong.

"I think that people who don't apologize because they honestly don't think they've done anything wrong, end up are more likely to end up benefiting than people who sort of like immediately turn over and show their bellies, and I don't know why that is," Katie Herzog told me. "But apologies are rarely accepted anyway." She never apologized for her article in *The Stranger* because she didn't think she had done anything wrong. "I think that was probably the smartest thing that I did." In her case, she says that perhaps it was less about principle and more a personality trait. "We should interview the parents of canceled people and find out how stubborn they were as children," she suggests, half-jokingly.

When I had a mob of angry female writers come after me, I had a choice to make. I could apologize and try to appease the mob by submitting to their requests, or I could refuse to bow down and accept whatever might come my way. Ultimately, I made the second choice. This wasn't simply a matter of stubbornness; I knew I was correct. In fact, my decision went against my people-pleasing, agreeable nature. Still, I didn't always have that certainty. I first had to grapple with the question: what if I'm wrong? I knew I was right in standing up for someone else. I knew that the way others behaved was abhorrent. But I cannot say that I had zero doubts along the way about how I chose to ultimately deal with the situation I inadvertently found myself in. It's difficult to have zero doubts when so many people are screaming at you about what an awful person you are. I would say I've never experienced such treatment before, but the situation echoed those moments when I was bullied and gossiped about in elementary and high school. For a while, I felt like a teenager again.

The self-doubt isn't so bad, Herzog tells me. "You should continually be inspecting that," she says, "That's one of the things that I think is important, and one of the lessons that I learned through this whole saga is that it's incredibly important to have some sort of epistemic humility." After all, people are wrong about things all the time. "It's so painful to admit the truth when you're wrong about something, but when you do [admit it, you gain esteem] . . . when you were genuinely wrong about something." But, she's quick to point out, that's very different from being coerced into an apology.

When I wrote the op-ed for *Newsweek* in which I shared my experience of being targeted, I was quite certain that I would be attacked again. Or rather, that the attacks would intensify. But that's not quite what happened. Although in private quarters, the mob did indeed discuss, mock, and attack the piece, I'm told, they never came after me directly again. At that point, I was too strong a target for them; I had already shown I wouldn't back down. Peter Boghossian agrees that this is the key. "They'll take any sign of weakness as an opportunity to sink their fangs in and just rip and shred," he says, not mincing any words. Part of what makes the mob so vitriolic and aggressive is their sense of righteousness. No matter how malicious the attacks, he adds, "They see something in themselves as virtuous as a consequence."

By touching on this idea, the article itself, titled "The Rise of Righteous Online Bullies," also offered some level of protection. By coming after me, the bullies would only be proving the point that I was making in that article—that bullying behavior "shuts down conversation, pushes us further apart, [and] alienates and prevents us from solving issues." I concluded with the line: "There's no better way to defeat a bully than to stand up and use your voice to fight back." The article itself served as a testament to this. So they moved on to someone else. Bullies always do.

The confidence with which I spoke was not false bluster. Having now gone through all the stages of emotional grief of this very public attack by the intolerant online mob (by people I had previously seen as colleagues), I was now equipped with a new kind of outlook. I learned to put things into perspective by looking at the situation this way: if I disagreed with someone about something, even a highly charged issue, how would I behave toward that person? That question gave me significant clarity. In fact, it turned everything around. My answer was: well, I would disagree, but I would never engage with someone the way that those people were acting toward me. That critical point of distinction made me look at the people attacking me in an entirely different way. At that point, I no longer felt like I owed it to them to engage or take them seriously—if that's the way they chose to communicate with me, through personal attacks and threats. But I would continue to consider the views of those who were respectful and polite in their disagreement.

Boghossian agrees that this is the right approach. In fact, he puts it more bluntly: "You must never apologize to the mob. I mean, never. In fact, if anything, apologizing to the mob will fuck you worse than anything . . . No matter what you say, it's never as bad as 'I'm sorry.' You think that you're sorry—that you're taking responsibility, right? Well, there is no redemption. This is a new religion, and privilege is the original sin. There's no redemption narrative in any of this stuff . . . so anytime you say, 'I'm sorry,' you're saying, I'm a Nazi. I'm a racist. I love Adolf Hitler—all of this craziness. It's just a mimetic ideology."

He says those who apologize to the bullies have a fundamental misunderstanding about how the mob works: "Why do you think people are so quick to say they're sorry? Because they think that if they say they're sorry, they will be forgiven. Then, they can get on with their lives. But in fact, it's the exact opposite thing that happens. It prevents you from getting on with your life." You're under no obligation to respond to somebody, let alone apologize to them, says Boghossian. "Why should you? You don't even know these people."

What is behind the phenomenon of devout apologists anyway? Certainly, for many, it comes from the desire to avoid conflict. Some are almost certainly aware that they haven't even done anything worth truly apologizing for but feel like they have no other choice lest they be cast out of society. Apologizing, even in the absence of a "crime," can be seen as a way of minimizing impact—as a defense from a greater attack. Many psychologists link this strategy to childhood experiences, particularly those within family environments where the child might have had to place their own needs below that of others. A low sense of self-worth reinforces this behavior. Then there's the desire to please people and be seen as good. The most self-serving apologists are those who turn it into a performance, those who even go as far as apologizing for the "sins" of others they've never even known or for their "privilege." These apologies serve no practical purpose other than to draw attention to the person apologizing—they are always done in front of an audience. The more prolific among them set an example with apologetic viral videos, statements, and even media tours. And because they have pre-apologized, they are safe, right?

Seen this way an apology as an act of public self-flagellation is an attempt to deter the mob in advance. As Jon Ronson points out in his book *So You've Been Publicly Shamed*, there are a lot of incentives for people to join pile-ons. The instant feedback loops are addictive.

The New Flagellants go along to get along, as the saying goes. It's a way of maintaining control. How can the bullies beat someone into submission when they've already submitted? After all, for those who don't keep up with the ever-evolving social codes, "judgment can be swift—and merciless," writes *The Atlantic*'s Anne Applebaum. In some religious practices, flagellation is the disciplinary or devotional practice of beating one's self with whips (or other tools)—a way toward purification. It's a form of punishment and penance. There's nothing inherently wrong with taking responsibility for wrong actions and providing those who have been wronged with an acknowledgment of that—that helps keep a healthy society and maintain good relationships—but the trouble arises when one apologizes excessively or without having done anything wrong in the first place. It doesn't make you appear nice; it makes you appear weak. It takes away your power. It sends the message that you can be abused. It makes you a target. And, perhaps worst of all, it makes you inauthentic to yourself and what you actually believe.

This is the realization Winston Marshall came to. Although he issued an apology, he quickly realized he had nothing to apologize for and withdrew it: "I think if you are not wrong, then you shouldn't apologize," he says. But, he adds, you should certainly be open to the possibility of being wrong. He gives the example of a dinner party: "You say something, and someone on the other side of the table is shocked. And you're like, 'Oh, I didn't realize I was saying something wrong. I'm sorry to offend you. Maybe you can explain to me what I've got wrong.' That's like a normal human reaction. And in that sense, I think it's okay to apologize. I'm not one of those sort of anti-apology people. But, on the other hand, there have been some apologies which are just beyond absurd."

The solution is clear: stay true to yourself in the face of unreasonable people and demands, but don't do so in a way that ends the chance of any further discussion or reconciliation. We need more conversations and less closing the door on them. In our increasingly polarized world, dissenting voices need to be heard and listened to, so it is more important than ever that we act in a careful and thoughtful manner that unifies rather than in a righteous and radical manner that divides. Model the behavior and attitudes you'd like to see. This includes always considering whether you might be wrong—no matter the situation or debate. That's not a sign of weakness; that's a sign of strength. But when you're not wrong, don't let fear silence you into submission. Always bear this in mind: when you've committed no wrongdoing, no one holds the authority to demand an apology from you, nor should you feel obliged to offer one. Stay firm, stay true. When your conscience is clear, don't be coerced or surrender your voice. Set it free.

And never apologize for this.

## Notes

The Applebaum quote comes from her essay "The New Puritans," *Atlantic*, August 31, 2021, www.theatlantic.com/magazine/archive/2021/10/new-puritans-mob-justice-canceled/619818.

For more on pile-ons and their real-world effects, see Jon Ronson, *So You've Been Publicly Shamed* (Picador, 2015).

For a story about bonds being formed among "Thought Criminals," see Emma Green, "The Party Is Cancelled," *New Yorker*, May 17, 2023, www.newyorker.com/news/our-local-correspondents/the-party-is-cancelled.

# Acknowledgments

To the people who take risks to do the right thing and speak the truth and defend others. Not because they are fearless but because they cannot act any other way and do so despite their fear. We are all first editions, all of us, so let's take better care of each other to ensure we are well-preserved through this journey we call life. To my family, who taught me how we can passionately disagree and still share a meal and still continue to support each other fully, as well as my closest friends, who have been there during the toughest moments and the joyful ones, too. To the people who think the best of me no matter what I say out loud because they know what's truly in my heart. To those who allow me to make mistakes. To my beloved dog, who taught me how to love unconditionally, whose presence I miss even all these years after her departure from the physical realm, and for whom I'll always carry my love. To those who have pain in their hearts, I hope you find peace and kindness. To those who haven't found your voice yet, I hope you find the courage in the moments when it matters most. Live your life with principles, so you owe . . . no apologies.

# Resources

Whatever you decide to do, it's important to know that you're not alone. Whether you're just interested in learning more, want to become part of a community, or need help to take on a case, there are a number of great organizations worth familiarizing yourself with. These are organizations that stand up for and protect free speech and promote discourse and bipartisanship.

### Foundation for Individual Rights and Expression

A nonprofit based in the United States, the Foundation for Individual Rights and Expression (FIRE) started out with the mission to defend and uphold the individual rights of students and faculty members on college and university campuses, expanding its initiatives into free speech advocacy and legal defense off-campus in 2022. In addition to public awareness campaigns, providing educational resources, and focusing on policy reforms, FIRE provides legal assistance to help combat instances of censorship and other restrictions on the free exchange of ideas. *thefire.org*

### Foundation Against Intolerance and Racism

The Foundation Against Intolerance and Racism (FAIR) is a nonpartisan organization committed to promoting civil rights and liberties, with the goal of fostering a shared pro-human culture that values fairness, understanding, and humanity. Through their work, FAIR strives to create an inclusive society that upholds the principles of equality and respects the rights of all individuals. They address issues in medicine, arts, education, and beyond. There are chapters to join across both the United States and Canada.

*fairforall.org*

## The Institute for Justice

A nonprofit public interest law firm that's dedicated to defending vital individual liberties from the abuses of government power and protecting constitutional rights.

*ij.org*

## Moral Courage

An unconventional DEI training program that rejects labeling people and defines "diversity" to include diversity of viewpoint. Their "Diversity Without Division" approach focuses on teaching people at companies, higher education, and K-12 institutions to turn contentious issues into constructive conversations.

*moralcourage.com*

## Street Epistemology

This is a great resource for those looking to learn more about Street Epistemology and how to practice it. The techniques developed through the practice of Street Epistemology allow people to apply philosophy and psychology-based tools to better reflect on their own reasoning, as well as use them to conduct civil conversations and assess whether one's confidence level in various claims being true is justified. The practice promotes critical thinking and encourages more reflections on our own beliefs, along with productive dialogue.

*streetepistemology.com*

## Institute for Liberal Values

The Institute for Liberal Values (ILV) is dedicated to promoting classical liberal values such as reason and freedom for the collective benefit of humanity. Their mission involves advocating for individuality, equal opportunities, freedom of expression, diversity of viewpoints, deliberative democracy, and the critical examination of all political and ethical assertions, regardless of their origin. To fulfill their mission, they focus on empowering individuals, communities, and organizations by providing them with the necessary skills and tools for creating a society that is dignified and empowered.

*ilvalues.org*

## Center for Inquiry

The Center for Inquiry (CFI) is a nonprofit organization that strives to foster a secular society based on reason, science, freedom of inquiry, and humanist values. It focuses on ensuring that science, facts, and critical thought guide public policy rather than pseudoscience or prejudice. Likewise, CFI embraces the ideal that freedom of expression should be enjoyed by all and that any idea can be open to

*centerforinquiry.org*

## Foundation for Freedom Online

The Foundation For Freedom Online (FFO) is an organization focused on safeguarding free speech and preserving the openness of the Internet. They are committed to their mission through the provision of educational reports, legal support, and analysis of public policies that pose risks to digital freedoms. Their aim is to offer impartial guidance and aid to individuals and communities who are advocating for the principles of freedom of speech, expression, and the unrestricted sharing of ideas in the online realm.

*foundationforfreedomonline.com*

## Braver Angels

Braver Angels is an organization dedicated to addressing the crisis of growing partisan animosity in the United States. As Americans on opposite sides of the political spectrum increasingly dislike one another, Braver Angels recognizes the threat this poses to the nation. The organization aims to bring Americans together, bridging the partisan divide and strengthening the democratic republic.

Through values of respect, humility, honesty, and responsible citizenship, Braver Angels seeks to foster an America where political disagreements are embraced with civility, allowing for the flourishing of civic friendship and the strengthening of the nation through diverse perspectives. Rather than attempting to change people's views on specific issues, Braver Angels focuses on changing their views of each other.

The organization promotes understanding by encouraging individuals to engage with opposing viewpoints, to seek common ground and opportunities for collaboration, and to create spaces for productive dialogue among those with differing opinions.

*braverangels.org*

## Bridge USA

As a nonprofit organization driven by youth leadership, its primary objective is to create inclusive spaces on high school and college campuses where students can engage in open discussions about political matters. The organization recognizes that political division stands as a significant challenge in the United States. Unfortunately, today's youth often receive the message that tribalism is superior to unity, and conversing across differences is deemed impossible. BridgeUSA firmly believes that this perception is incorrect.

In 2016, BridgeUSA was established in response to the escalating polarization observed on university campuses. Their efforts focus on cultivating empathy and understanding, fostering ideological diversity, and promoting solution-oriented politics. By facilitating constructive dia-

logues among America's youth, the organization strives to equip the upcoming generation of leaders with the necessary skills to navigate conflicts, discover resolutions that transcend differences, and build bridges
within their communities.

Presently, BridgeUSA operates on more than 50 college campuses
and 24 high school campuses across the United States.
*bridgeusa.org*

## Tangle

Tangle is an independent, nonpartisan politics newsletter. We summa-
rize the best arguments from across the political spectrum on the news
of the day.
*readtangle.com*

## Arc Digital

An independent media site committed to intellectual pluralism and providing a platform for a diverse range of perspectives, as well as insightful
analysis and commentary on a wide range of topics such as politics, policy, social issues, culture, world affairs, economics, science, technology,
philosophy, and more.
*arcdigital.media*

## The Center for Humane Technology

The Center for Humane Technology (CHT) is an independent nonprofit organization with a mission to steer technology toward a more
humane future that prioritizes our well-being, democratic functioning,
and the integrity of our shared information environment. It all began in
2013 when Tristan Harris, a former Google Design Ethicist, delivered a
compelling presentation titled "A Call to Minimize Distraction & Respect Users' Attention," which gained viral attention. This presentation,
along with subsequent TED talks and a 60 Minutes interview, ignited
the Time Well Spent movement. In 2018, CHT was established as a

501(c)(3) nonprofit, building upon the foundation laid by the movement to address the ethical concerns surrounding technology and its impact on society.

*humanetech.com*

## The Munk Debates

As discourse becomes increasingly polarized, the Munk Debates are dedicated to reviving the art of civil and substantive public debate. Since 2008, they've been bringing together renowned figures such as Stephen Fry, Christopher Hitchens, Henry Kissinger, and Jordan Peterson to participate in debates on significant contemporary issues in the belief that such conversations are crucial for the public good. These debates are hosted in Toronto, Canada. In addition, the organization also has a one-on-one debate podcast, the Munk Dialogues series, and other valuable content.

*munkdebates.com*

## Heterodox Academy

Heterodox Academy (HxA) is an impartial and nonprofit membership organization consisting of a vast community of faculty, staff, and students. Their collective mission is to promote the values of open inquiry, viewpoint diversity, and constructive disagreement in order to enhance higher education and academic research. With thousands of members, HxA is dedicated to advancing these principles and fostering an environment that encourages a wide range of perspectives and respectful discourse within educational institutions.

*heterodoxacademy.org*

# About the Author

Katherine Brodsky is a commentator and writer who has contributed to publications such as *Newsweek, Variety, WIRED, Washington Post, Guardian, Esquire, CNN.com, Vulture, Playboy, Independent, Mashable,* and many others—covering a diverse range of topics from culture to tech. She posts as @mysteriouskat on X and regularly publishes essays on her Substack *Random Minds* (randomminds.substack.com).